FREEDOM FROM S.I.N.
Satan's Intended Notion

STUDY GUIDE
To be used in conjunction with the book

By
Lawrence P. Luby

Published by HIS Publishing Group, Dallas, Texas 75225
Division of Human Improvement Specialists, llc
For Information Visit: hispublishinggroup.com
Or Contact: info@hispublishinggroup.com

Please visit our book site to purchase materials: freedomfromsin.net
Contact: info@freedomfromsin.net

Copyright © 2008 by Lawrence P. Luby. All rights reserved.
Permission is granted to reproduce twenty-five copies for small group study.
Permission to reproduce or transmit additional copies in any form or by any means, electronic or mechanical, including photocopying and recording, or by any information storage and retrieval system, must be obtained in writing from the author.
Visit Lawrence P. Luby at his web site: mtoleadership.com
Contact: info@mtoleadership.com

Cover design by Ty Walsworth at Culture Red
Visit the website: culture-red.com

All scripture quoted in this book is from the New King James Version. "Scripture taken from the New King James Version. Copyright © 1982 by Thomas Nelson, Inc. Used by permission. All rights reserved."

ISBN-13: 978-0-615-35710-2
Printed in the United States of America

Contents

INTRODUCTION		5
FACILITATOR GUIDE		7
WEEKLY FACILITATOR OUTLINES		11
PARTICIPANT GUIDE		23

WEEK I   INTRODUCTION / THE TRINITY: The Godhead — 25
  DAY ONE — Introduction / Trinity
  DAY TWO — Role of John the Baptist
  DAY THREE — Attributes of God
  DAY FOUR — Holy Spirit and the Infinite Nature of God's creation
  DAY FIVE — Ways we Reject God and Consequences for Rejecting God

WEEK II   SATAN'S INTENDED NOTION — 35
  DAY ONE — Society Defined
  DAY TWO — Gang Formation
  DAY THREE — True Intentions
  DAY FOUR — Jesus Christ
  DAY FIVE — History

WEEK III   THE SET-UP — 45
  DAY ONE — Satan's Role in History
  DAY TWO — Original Sin
  DAY THREE — Temptation of Man
  DAY FOUR — Forsaking Authority
  DAY FIVE — Separation from God

WEEK IV   SOCIETAL ADDICTION — 55
  DAY ONE — The Addictive Process
  DAY TWO — Roots of Addiction
  DAY THREE — Cycle of Addiction
  DAY FOUR — Addictive Erosion
  DAY FIVE — Freedom from Addiction

WEEK V   PLAYING LIFE — 65
  DAY ONE — Running with the Herd / Pick and Choose to Suit
  DAY TWO — Pick and Choose to Suit (continued)
  DAY THREE — To Pull or To Push / Satan's Playbook
  DAY FOUR — Satan's Playbook (continued)
  DAY FIVE — The Armor of God

Contents

WEEK VI   CLIMACTIC DELIVERANCE   77
    DAY ONE — Quick Fix
    DAY TWO — Entitlement
    DAY THREE — The Truth about Deliverance / True Deliverance
    DAY FOUR — True Deliverance (continued)
    DAY FIVE — Four Keys to the Kingdom

WEEK VII   STAIRWAY TO HEAVEN   89
    DAY ONE — Acknowledgement and Acceptance
    DAY TWO — Conversion and Brokenness
    DAY THREE — Restoration and Repentance
    DAY FOUR — Purification and Eternal Salvation
    DAY FIVE — Ministry

WEEK VIII   PRACTICE ROUNDS   101
    DAY ONE — Biblical Practice Rounds
    DAY TWO — Life of Joseph
    DAY THREE — Life of Joseph (continued)
    DAY FOUR — Relational Practice Rounds / Vocational Practice Rounds
    DAY FIVE — Practice Rounds of Endurance / Unexpected Practice Rounds

WEEK IX   CONCLUSION   113
    DAY ONE — God's Picture Puzzle
    DAY TWO — God's Picture Puzzle (continued)
    DAY THREE — Placing the Trinity Over Our Lives
    DAY FOUR — Final Review
    DAY FIVE — iUC Questionnaire

INTRODUCTION

I pray, as you participate in this study, God will draw you into a more intimate relationship with Him and free you of any hold that S.I.N. has placed on your life. It is my desire that you would be propelled on your spiritual journey in preparation for eternal life with our Creator.

Your Freedom to be experienced as an outcome of this study will be in direct proportion with your level of input. I encourage you to embrace the concepts contained herein and challenge you to search the scriptures letting the Word of God bring to life the freedom the Holy Spirit desires for you.

The material offered in the book and in this study is a result of the passion God placed on my heart over ten years ago. I believe the strategic timing and delivery of this material is in accordance with His will. Given the political and social climate of our times, this study might very well be one of the most life changing experiences of your life.

We have been born for such a time as this and must take up the fight and stand against the spiritual enemy bent on destroying our societal structure and dragging as many with him into an eternity separated from God.

For believers the final victory is ours, for one day we will look out over eternity and declare our "Freedom from S.I.N."

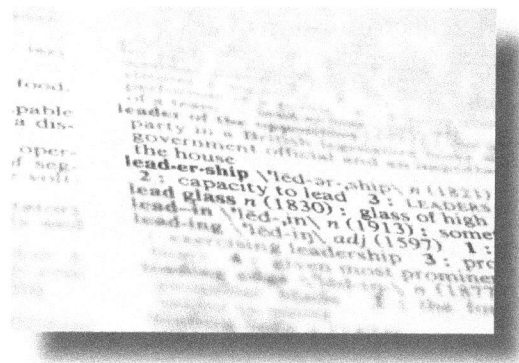

FACILITATOR GUIDE

OVERVIEW

It is important to be prepared prior to beginning the study. Spend the week before your scheduled Sunday school class or small-group study by praying and fasting. If possible, encourage the participants to do the same.

Be sure to read the book and work through the guide each week taking notes of the main points you want to cover. We have provided a list of suggested questions to help you prepare each week. Remain flexible, but know in advance which questions you think would be best for your group. It is important to let the Holy Spirit guide your time together.

Have your roster filled out with those who will attend. Get to know the names of your participants. Knowing their names makes them feel important and will help you to move the discussions along in a timely manner.

Speak with your participants and get to know them before beginning your time together. It will be important to know their spiritual condition. For example, if you know you will be leading a group of mature and seasoned Christians, you are encouraged to spend more time in interactive discussion. If on the other hand, you are leading a mixed group or spiritually new group, you want to be prepared to facilitate the process effectively.

PROCESS

The study is led by a facilitator, and the participants absorb the material through their personal involvement in discussions and working through the questions each week. This facilitated learning process is designed to assist participants in covering one chapter of the book each week; each chapter is broken down in a five-day format.

As the facilitator, you are encouraged to provide a safe and shared environment for the promotion of ideas and learning based on the principles offered in the Bible. Your role is to make the study process easier by providing structure, guidance and a safe environment for those in attendance.

You are to be more concerned about what is discussed and how the questions are discussed than having all the answers. In fact, it is best if you limit your involvement by not interjecting or participating in discussions. However, your source is the Word and when in doubt about the answer to a question always refer back to the Word and reflect questions back on the group instead of answering.

Your primary function as the facilitator is to be a guide, assisting participants to reach in and pull out the answers that reside in each of them. Your confident attitude and seriousness of purpose will set the tone for the discussions and the learning that takes place. You always want to appear interested and enthusiastic as you lead them on their journey to freedom.

MATERIALS

You are granted permission to copy up to twenty-five copies of this study guide for your participants. We base this solely on the honor system. Answers to the guide may be found on the author website at www.freedomfromsin.net.

Provide a three-ring binder for each participant. Include in the binder the Participant's Guide and material for the first week. It is vitally important to copy only one week at a time. This facilitates a process that will assist your participants to focus on the material you will be covering in your group time together.

- Roster (Have blanks for keeping roll each week)
- Name Tags
- Copies of the Book
- Leaders Guide
- Copies of the Study Guide
- Three-ring binders for participant copies
- Bible (Have extras on hand for those who forget to bring one)
- Journal (For prayer requests and other information)
- Tri-pod and chart (Post questions so they remain visible during discussions)
- Pens and highlighters
- Optional: Music is optional—having christian music playing in the background will help set the proper tone for your time together.
- Optional: Answers to the Study Guide printed from website

SUGGESTED FORMAT FOR GROUP SESSIONS—approximately 60 minutes

5 Minutes—Introduction and Opening Prayer
20 Minutes—Quick Daily Review (Guide should have been completed prior to class)
30 Minutes—Interactive Discussion (Present 2-3 questions depending on time)
5 Minutes—Closing Prayer and Prayer Requests

ROOM SET-UP

The arrangement of tables and chairs is important and plays a role in the effectiveness of the material being covered. Participants should be facing one another. Therefore forming a circle is most conducive to open discussion. At a minimum, encourage participants to turn toward and address the group when engaged in discussion.

Secure the room as much as possible by closing doors, turning off the background music and adjusting the lights to provide an adequate interactive environment. Ask participants to turn off cell phones and pagers. Let everyone know where the restrooms are and ask them to be respectful when leaving or returning to the group.

FACILITATING TIPS

- Start on time, end on time.
- Do not preach, lecture or attempt to persuade others to your way of thinking.
- Do not scold, embarrass, or make fun about any of the participants.
- Know the names of the participants.
- Ask additional questions to keep the discussion flowing.
- Be attentive to the different personalities within the group, encourage participation and respect within the group.
- Avoid being drawn into the right or wrong of an issue.
- Smile and use good eye contact when addressing participants.
- Do not play expert even if you are extremely well educated in the subject matter.
- When asked a question, repeat the question and ask the group for their input.
- Maintain an adequate flow to remain within your intended time limits.
- Disagreements can be constructive or destructive. This will depend on the issue and how the situation is handled. You want to encourage debate, but also encourage participants to respect the group's time. Avoid rebukes, it is always better to address the statement or comment rather than the individual.
- Be flexible and remember the Holy Spirit is directing your time together.

CONFIDENTIALITY

Share the importance of respecting one another's anonymity. Explain the meaning of the statement, "What is said in the group, stays in the group."

Encourage them, in order to build trust and confidence, how it is important to respect each individual and not to disclose information that is shared in the group with anyone outside the group. This will facilitate deeper and more personal interactive discussions.

BEFORE EACH SESSION

Read and work through the material for that week. Pray about the most important points you want to cover. Much will depend on the spiritual maturity of the group. Prepare an outline including times for the material you want to cover and the questions for group discussion. Remember, the participants should have worked through the material, so it is not important to cover every topic. Start on time and end on time.

DURING THE SESSION

Open in prayer and invite the Lord's presence. Remember your role is that of a facilitator. It is imperative to remain spiritually minded and flexible, but at the same time be keenly aware of your remaining time and the material to cover. However, there is no need to rush through the material. It is more important for the Holy Spirit to guide your time together.

Questions are woven into the material each week. Participants are encouraged to be prepared to discuss these during the group session. Your role should not be to answer every question. If a question or discussion is presented, we encourage you to reflect it back to the group by asking what they think. As a facilitator, you do not want to be perceived as the expert, but as the guide. This is the biggest challenge in leading a group and takes maturity and discipline on the part of the facilitator.

It is your responsibility to be aware of the dynamics of the group and keep the flow. There will be participants who will tend to dominate the discussions, make it your goal to maintain the flow out of respect for the whole group. You also want to be aware of participants who tend to be introverted or guarded. Try to encourage their involvement by asking their thoughts about a particular subject or question. Avoid the trap of being drawn into a discussion of right and wrong. Remember everyone is right and everyone is wrong. You want to maintain the attitude that says, "What can we learn and take away from the discussion?"

AFTER THE SESSION

Maintain a journal over the course of the study, this will assist you in keeping track of specific prayer requests and other information presented in the class. It also sets a good example for those you are leading. Encourage participants to keep their own journal and to pray for one another before your next session.

RESPONSE TO GOD'S ROLE IN YOUR GROUP

- Trust the Holy Spirit to guide you when He wants to work in and through your group.
- Lay down your agenda and give freedom for the Holy Spirit to move each week.
- Be spiritually sensitive to the needs of the group.
- Be attentive to the members in attendance and be ready to engage them in the discussions. However, please do not pressure anyone to participate outside of his or her will.
- Encourage testimonies throughout the study: what the participants feel God is doing through their time in the group and the material presented each week.
- Remember most of all to have fun and create an enjoyable atmosphere.

WEEKLY FACILITATOR OUTLINES

WEEK I - INTRODUCTION
THE TRINITY: The Godhead

Introduction and opening prayer: 5 minutes

Invite the presence of the Holy Spirit

Weekly Review: 20 minutes

- What does it mean to be born into sin?
- Discuss the three parts of the Trinity. Compare the three parts of the Trinity with the word, light and life. (John 1:1-5 pg. 16 / Definition of Trinity pg. 17)
- What was John's baptism? What was Jesus' baptism? (John 1:29-31 pg. 17 / John 1:32-34 pg. 18 & Matthew 3:11 Pg. 18)
- Did Jesus claim to be God? (John 10:25-30 pg 20)
- What are the three divine personalities of God and how are they defined? (Jeremiah 32:17-18, Psalm 139:7-12 pg. 23 & John 4:24 pg 23)
- How does the trinity compare to the CEO, President and team members of a company? (Philippians 2:6-7 pg. 23 & John 14:26 pg. 23)
- How does the Holy Spirit bring conviction into our hearts? (John 14:26 pg. 23)
- Did Jesus speak on His own authority? Who's authority? (John 5:19 pg. 29)
- What does it mean to be a co-creator with God of our own children? (Galatians 4:1-7 pg. 30)
- Discuss God in terms of the Alpha and Omega. (Revelation 1:8 pg. 31)
- Why doesn't anyone know the date of Christ's return? (Matthew 24:36 pg. 34)
- Is creation a concept birthed from man's understanding?
- What are we risking when we reject God? (Hebrews 13:8-9 pg. 34)
- What three things does God give all of us?

Interactive Discussion Questions: 30 minutes

1) What are your thoughts and beliefs about the accuracy of the bible?
2) Relate times you have cried out to God or to an unknown creator? Describe your experience.
3) Discuss the difference in the baptisms of John and the baptism of Jesus Christ as mentioned in Matthew 3:11 on page 18 in the book.
4) Can the created fully understand the creator?
5) Does your spirit live on for all eternity? Share your thoughts and opinions on how your spirit lives on.
6) Open a discussion about John 14:6-Jesus said to him, "I am the way, the truth, and the life. No one comes to the Father except through Me."

Close in Prayer: 5 minutes

Week II - Satan's Intended Notion

Introduction and opening prayer: 5 minutes

Invite the presence of the Holy Spirit

Weekly Review: 20 minutes

- How has S.I.N. become Societal in Nature? (Revelation 12:9, Luke 10:18 & John 10:10 pg. 37)
- What is the difference between a spiritual valley and a spiritual mountaintop?
- What does it mean to be spiritually mature?
- Does our spiritual enemy care about right or wrong? Briefly Discuss.
- How do our peers and the groups we associate with influence our life?
- How are gangs formed? Name some of the negative influences gangs have on society. (Definition pg. 42)
- What is a super predator? (Definition pg. 45)
- How did Christ build His team and in what way was it similar to the theory of gang formation? (Ecclesiastes 4:9-12 pg. 46) &, (John 1:35-39 & John 1:40-53 pg. 53 & 54)
- Why is the intention of the heart so important? (Matthew 12:34-35, 1 Corinthians 4:5, Proverbs 14:10-14 & Hebrews 10:22 (page 56)
- Is it okay to lie, deceive or falsely miss-lead others? Could this be indicative of a deceptive spirit at work?
- What was Jesus' intention? How does that differ with many of the societal intentions we are faced with today? (Deuteronomy 6:5 pg. 57)
- What three branches of the government did our Founding Fathers set up to preserve the free will of the people? (pg. 58)
- What does it mean that Jesus is the head of the body? (Colossians 1:15-20 pg. 59)

Interactive Discussion Questions: 30 minutes

1) Discuss some ways you have experienced spiritual erosion and societal erosion.
2) What is the parallel between spiritual erosion and societal erosion?
3) What is the climate of your social circles? Are they healthy, loving and life building?
4) How you can invite the Holy Spirit to be the third cord in your life?
5) Discuss a time when someone with an ill-intended heart, has attempted to take advantage of you.
6) What are some spiritual principles our Founding Father's used to establish the foundation of our country.

Close in Prayer: 5 minutes

WEEK III - THE SET-UP

Introduction and opening prayer: 5 minutes

Invite the presence of the Holy Spirit

Weekly Review: 20 minutes

- Where does the enemy reside?
- Did Lucifer have free will and choice in what to believe? (Isaiah 14:12, 2 Corinthians 11:14 & Isaiah 14:13-14 pg. 62)
- Did God expect Satan to rebel? (Ezekiel 28:15 pg. 64)
- Does God expect us to rebel?
- Why didn't God just do away with Satan and his rebellious angels?
- Who did God grant dominion over the earth?
  (Genesis 1:26 & Genesis 1:27-28 pg. 65 and 66)
- How did Satan "Set-Up" mankind and attempt to unseat God from His throne?
- What is Satan's ultimate eternal fate? What is meant by the second death?
- What was God's command to Adam in the garden?
  (Genesis 2:8-9 & Genesis 2:16-17 pg. 70)
- How did Satan twist the truth and make sin sound appealing? (Genesis 3:1-5 pg. 72)
- What spiritual role was Adam to exercise with Eve? Are men still guilty today? (Ephesians 5:25 & Ephesians 5:33 pg. 74)
- Because of sin what did Cain do? What would have been the outcome had he heeded God's advice? (Genesis 4:6-10 pg. 77)
- What is spiritual death? (Read Revelation 1:18 pg. 79)
- What does sin bring into our family and our relationships?
- How do we keep from giving in to the lust of the flesh, lust of the eyes and the pride of life? (Romans 5:19 – 21 & 1 John 2:16 pg. 83 & 84)

Interactive Discussion Questions: 30 minute

1) Based on the stories at the beginning of Chapter 3, discuss what kind of life these children are destined to have.
2) Discuss the true meaning of unconditional love.
3) Discuss some ways we are still eating from the "Tree of the knowledge of good and evil."
4) How could we really know what determines functional if society sets the functional and dysfunctional standard?
5) Did your Mother and Father follow Proverbs 1:8 in your family? Are you following it in your family?

Close in Prayer: 5 minutes

Week IV - Societal Addiction

Introduction and opening prayer: 5 minutes

Invite the presence of the Holy Spirit

Weekly Review: 20 minutes

- How has Satan used material possessions to mold our society?
- How do we maintain the proper spiritual balance in our lives? (Matthew 6: 31-34 pg. 85 & 86)
- What does the statement mean, "Society teaches the opposite of what God teaches"?
- What does deception cause? (Jeremiah 17:9-10 pg. 87)
- How are we influenced by the world around us?
- What is meant by trash in—trash out?
- What are some of the ways roots of addiction become manifested in our lives?
- Where do these roots stem from? (Mark 7:14-23 pg. 88)
- What was the root of Eve's addiction and how was it manifested?
- Is there a cycle to the addictive process? How does our advertising contribute to this cycle?
- Has alcohol or any other mind-altering substance had a positive influence on your life? (story on pg. 90)
- What are some ways parenting could be improved if alcohol wasn't in the home?
- What is meant by addictive erosion? (defined on pg. 95)
- How has the enemy used the loosening of our moral values to attack our society?
- What is the only true way to break free from the bondage of addiction? (Luke 10:19-20 pg. 97)
- Where does our spirit go when we die? (Genesis 2:7 & Ecclesiastes 12:7 pg. 101)
- What do the clouds of ignorance shroud? (Jeremiah 1:4-5 & Matthew 26:26-28 pg. 102 & 103)

Interactive Discussion Questions: 30 minute

1) What does the "American Dream," mean to you? How has the dream been distorted in today's environment?
2) What are some ways we have become addicted to our surroundings?
3) Are there roots still active in your life?
4) What are some areas where you see addictive erosion occurring in our society?
5) Discuss 2 Peter 3:8—"But, beloved, do not forget this one thing, that with the Lord one day is as a thousand years, and a thousand years as one day."

Close in Prayer: 5 minutes

WEEK V - PLAYING LIFE

Introduction and opening prayer: 5 minutes

Invite the presence of the Holy Spirit

Weekly Review: 20 minutes

- Does your life have purpose and meaning?
  (Proverbs 20:18, Proverbs 21:5 & Proverbs 21:11 pg. 106)
- Is there a tendency among christians today to pick portions of scripture to justify their lifestyles? Why is this dangerous?
- What happens inside us when we truly make a heartfelt decision to follow the Word of God?
- Did Jesus give us permission to continue our sinful behavior? (1 John 2:1, Romans 7:17 & Romans 6:1 pg. 108)
- Is the law negated once we accept Christ' death and resurrection? (613 Mitzvos pg. 259)
- What does it mean in Romans 5 when Paul says, "where sin abounds grace abounds much more"? (Romans 5:18-21 pg. 111)
- What are some examples of willful sin? (1 Corinthians 6:9-10 pg. 113)
- Who is our ultimate judge? Will we be able to escape eternal judgment?
  (Matthew 7:1-3 pg. 114)
- What is the spiritual principle behind "To Pull or to Push"? (stories 115 & 116)
- Will knowing the enemy's playbook give us an advantage in life? (Proverbs 1:7 pg. 117)
- What was God's instruction to Cain about sin? (Genesis 4:6-7 pg. 118)
- What carries us in our time of weakness? (2 Corinthians 12: 9-10 pg. 121)
- What is our reward for overcoming temptation? (James 1:12 pg. 124)
- Are we to engage the enemy's attacks or defend against his lies?
  (Matthew 27:11-14 pg. 124)
- How do you put on the armor of God in your daily life? What is the most important aspect of putting on the armor of God? (Ephesians 6:10-17 pg. 130)
- What are some of the vessels the enemy uses to attack us?

Interactive Discussion Questions: 30 minute

1) Not Optional—Recite the Ten Commandments * (Exodus 20:3-17 pg. 119 & 120)
2) Are we preparing for the mission we were put here on earth to achieve?
3) Have you become prey to complacency? Where you ran the risk or had a tendency to choose counsel that provided the easiest route in life, even if you sensed it was the wrong route?
4) Have you been drawn in to an area of sin innocently, only to linger long enough that later you felt further enticed to explore that area of sin in more depth? Where did it lead you?
5) Look back on your life and see if you can identify how the enemy has attacked you with his three primary plays: temptation, accusation & deception.

Close in Prayer: 5 minutes

Week VI - Climactic Deliverance

Introduction and opening prayer: 5 minutes

Invite the presence of the Holy Spirit

Weekly Review: 20 minutes

- Is eternal deliverance available to us all? How does eternal deliverance differ from a quick fix? (Proverbs 20:21 pg. 139)
- How do parents' unknowingly set their children up for spiritual hardship? (story pg. 140 & 141)
- What is the law of entitlement? How has it become a danger to our society? (Luke 15:24 pg. 145)
- How did society in the aftermath of WWII and Vietnam distort the idea of entitlement and what were the differences? (see 146 & 147)
- Why does it take time for something to have the proper sustaining impact in our life? (1 John 2:15-17 pg. 150)
- Does S.I.N. lie in wait to destroy us spiritually? (1 Peter 5:8 pg. 153)
- What does it mean in 1 Peter to "Be sober and vigilant"?
- What was Jesus' instruction to Nicodemus? (Read John 3:1-3 pg. 153 & John 3:4-10 pg. 154 & 155)
- Will being good grant you access into Heaven? Why or why not? (Luke 18:18 – 19 & Proverbs 20:6 pg. 157)
- In order to have true deliverance we must trust in Jesus Christ. What are the two primary requisites indicating you have eternal salvation? (John 5:24 & Romans 10:9-10 pg. 159)
- What is the spiritual significance of baptism?
- What is the danger of continuing in willful sin after being "Born again"? (Hebrews 10:26-29 pg. 162)
- What are the keys to the Kingdom? How do they help us to mature spiritually? (pg. 162-165)

Interactive Discussion Questions: 30 minute

Not Optional—ask the question below and solicit responses from the group: Do not assume everyone in your class has made a personal decision or that they have been water baptized. Use the bulleted list depending on his or her answers to the question. *

If you died and went to Heaven and the Lord just happened to be standing at the gate the very moment of your arrival and asked, "Son/Daughter why should I let you in?" What would your answer be?"

- If someone has not made a personal decision to accept Jesus Christ as his or her Lord and Savior, I encourage you to lead them in the prayer found on page 159. If they feel led by the Spirit, ask them to drop to their knees before God and pray the prayer aloud. Set their spiritual compass!

WEEK VI (continued)

- Maybe they have already prayed, but feel led to renew their commitment to the Lordship of Jesus Christ. Guide them by asking them to pray aloud to re-acknowledge Jesus Christ as their Lord and Savior, and commit to serve the Lord for the rest of their natural life. Reset their spiritual compass!
- Ask if everyone has been water baptized. Make arrangements with your church staff for anyone who would like to be baptized

Additional Questions if time allows:

1) Have you taken an inventory lately of your life, where you might possibly be turning away from God the Father? Are there any areas of your life that you need to turn back over to Him?
2) Talk about the quote by Phillips Brooks found on page 149 and how it still applies today.
3) When and how do you spend your quiet time with the Lord

* **Notes:** Be sure to journal any new decisions and share with your Pastoral leaders so proper follow up can be initiated.

Close in Prayer: 5 minutes

WEEK VII - STAIRWAY TO HEAVEN

Introduction and opening prayer: 5 minutes

Invite the presence of the Holy Spirit

Weekly Review: 20 minutes

- How is our spiritual journey like riding an escalator? (Proverbs 15:24 pg. 168)
- Review the steps on God's stairway to heaven. (pg. 168 & 169)
- How did Paul's Damascus road experience relate to these steps? (Acts 9:1-19)
- Does God's escalator ever break down? Can someone remove you from God's stairway? (John 10:29-30 pg. 177)
- Why is brokenness a step on God's stairway? Can we skip this step on our spiritual ascent? (John 10:29-30 pg. 177)
- Will God still reveal himself to us in the midst of our rejection and rebellion? (Hebrews 13:5 pg. 179)
- What bearing do our previous addictive choices have on our journey?
- What are the two things that a fool despises? (Proverbs 1:7 page 182)
- What are some of the ways we medicate our pain? (2 Timothy 3:1-7 pg. 183)
- How can we relate to Peter's experience on the night of Jesus' betrayal? (John 21:14-19 pg. 187)
- What are some good examples of the purification process at work in our lives? (John 17:19 pg. 188)
- What are some ways that we become conformed to the image of Christ? (Romans 8:29 pg. 190)
- What are the three areas of ministry Jesus refers to in the Great Commission? (Matthew 28:18-21 pg. 190)
- Do we all have a role to play in the church? (1 Corinthians 12:12, 18, James 1:17 & 1 Corinthians 12:20-21 pg. 194 & 195)
- What does it mean to step into the eternal realm? (Revelation 21:4, Revelation 21:10-21 & Luke 23:42-43 pg. 196 & 197)

Interactive Discussion Questions: 30 minute

1) Do you remember going to the mall as a child and riding the escalators? Did you ever try to go the opposite direction on the escalators? Have you ever tried running down an up escalator? How is this relevant to your spiritual walk with the Lord?
2) Has there been a time in your life where you were practicing the same behavior in life, expecting a different result?
3) What are some of the ways you see Timothy's warnings present in your surroundings? (2 Timothy 3:1-7 pg. 183)
4) Have there been times where you have struggled with God's answer or seeming lack of an answer to your prayers?
5) What are some ways you are involved in the work of ministry? What are some ways you could be more involved in the work of ministry?

Close in Prayer: 5 minutes

WEEK VIII - PRACTICE ROUNDS

Introduction and opening prayer: 5 minutes

Invite the presence of the Holy Spirit

Weekly Review: 20 minutes

    (Corinthians 9:24-25, Matthew 25:21 pg. 200 & 201)
- Discus how our life experiences are practice rounds in preparation for the future?
- What important benefit do our practice rounds hold for others?
- Were Joseph's practice rounds fair or merited in the eyes of the world? (pg. 203-213)
- Did Joseph excel wherever his practice rounds led him?
- How many years did Joseph spend practicing for God's purpose? (Genesis 41:39-42 pg. 210)
- What was that purpose? (Genesis 45:3-8 & Genesis 46:1-4 pg. 212 & 213)
- Can we fully comprehend the Lord's ways? What are we called to do?
- Is the calling on your life irrevocable? How do we know this? (Romans 11:29 pg. 216)
- Were there other men and women in the bible that endured such practice rounds? (page 217 & 218)
- What is the one thing they all had in common that helped them change the world?
- What are two of the biggest decisions we make in our lifetime? (page 218)
- What is the best way to look at seemingly missed opportunities? (Revelation 3:8 page 222)
- What is the one thing about the Lord we can trust?
- What happens when we lose our vision or we give up in life? (Proverbs 29:18 pg. 223)
- How do we endure through the good times and the hard times? (Proverbs 3:5-6 pg. 226)
- Who coaches us through the Lord's rulebook as we experience the practice rounds of life?

Interactive Discussion Questions: 30 minute

    Not Optional — Please review the actions taken, resulting consequences and lessons learned from the story about Joseph's life found on pages 214-216

Additional Questions if time allows:
1) Give examples of the relational practice rounds you have experienced.
2) Give examples of vocational practice rounds you have experienced.
3) Give examples of practice rounds of endurance you have experienced.
4) Give examples of unexpected practice rounds you have experienced.

Close in Prayer: 5 minutes

WEEK IX - CONCLUSION

Introduction and opening prayer: 5 minutes

Invite the presence of the Holy Spirit

Weekly Review: 20 minutes

- Do we truly believe that we have a piece in God's eternal puzzle? (pg. 229)
- How many members make up a family? (pg. 230)
- What do we learn through the family structure? (1 Peter 5:1-5 & 1 pg. 231)
- Does everyone have a part or a role to play in the family structure?
- Who did Jesus say were the members of His spiritual family? (Mark 3:33 pg. 233)
- As leaders, will we be held accountable how we functioned within the family? (Luke 9:49-50 & Matthew 7:21-23 pg. 235)
- Why is the concept of the tithe so controversial in our society? (Malachi 3:8-12 & Matthew 23:23-25 pg. 236 & 237)
- How does Satan keep us in bondage when put our possessions before or relationship with God? (Mark 12:41-44 pg. 237)
- What does it mean to be a cheerful giver? (2 Corinthians 9:7 pg. 238)
- How did George Washington express the importance of giving? What do you think he meant by this statement? (pg. 238)
- What benefit do we receive by placing the Trinity over our lives? (pg. 239)
- What are God's thoughts toward us and what does He desire to give us? (Jeremiah 29:11 pg. 242)
- What does it really mean to keep the end in mind? (pg. 245)

Interactive Discussion Questions: 30 minute

Not Optional — Discuss the results of the survey and the importance of knowing and embracing the primary qualities God created in each of us. *

Additional Questions if time allows:
1) What role has God called you to play in spiritual family? Why are there pieces missing in our family puzzles?
2) Why is there so much division within our natural families, our spiritual families and our societal families?
3) What are some examples of how a natural or spiritual family can get out of balance?
4) What are some ways we can place the Trinity over our lives?

* **Notes:** Cover the importance of getting in touch with their innately unique qualities and encourage each person in your group to focus on them daily.

If anyone in your group would like assistance in the discovery process or would like to explore his or her uniqueness in more depth, personal guidance and coaching is available from the author. Please have them contact info@mtoleadership.com to get more information and to set an appointment.

Close in Prayer: 5 minutes

PARTICIPANT GUIDE

OVERVIEW

It is important to be prepared prior to beginning the study. Spend the week before your scheduled Sunday school class or small-group study by praying and fasting. Be sure to read the book and work through the guide provided each week making notes of any of the main points you want to discuss in class.

The study guide is designed to assist you in covering one chapter of the book each week. Each chapter is broken down in a five-day format.

If available, obtain a roster from the leader in order to learn the names of those who will attend.

MATERIALS

- Completed copy of the Study Guide for that week
- Bible
- Journal *
- Pen
- Highlighter

* You are encouraged to journal what the Lord is showing you each week and to log prayer requests and other information.

BEFORE EACH SESSION

Read and work through the material for that week. Pray over your fellow participants, specific prayer requests and any other items the Lord puts on your heart. Be prepared to discuss the material presented and any specific questions for that week. The better prepared you are the more you and the other participants will get out of your time together.

DURING THE SESSION

During the opening prayer, join with your group leader to invite the Lord's presence. Please be spiritually minded and flexible. Be respectful of the other participants; it is important that everyone gets a chance to share. Knowing there is allotted time for each segment is important so you can be aware of the flow and assist the leader. We encourage you to participate in the interactive discussions, please limit your response time to be to respectful to others who want to share. We are not suggesting you rush through the material; it is more important for the Holy Spirit to guide your time together.

AFTER THE SESSION

Keep a journal each week and log the prayer requests of the group. Encourage each of your classmates to stay in contact throughout the week and to pray for one another. Be prepared to share anything the Lord has shown you through your time together and the material presented.

CONFIDENTIALITY

It is extremely important to respect one another's anonymity. Please do not share anything personal discussed within the group with anyone outside the group. This will give everyone more confidence to open up during the interactive discussions and make it easier for the Holy Spirit to guide your time together.

WEEK I
INTRODUCTION
THE TRINITY: The Godhead

DAY ONE — Introduction / Trinity

Open in Prayer — Invite the presence of the Holy Spirit

The title *Freedom from S.I.N.* stands for Freedom from Satan's Intended Notion, which has become Societal in Nature. The enemy has attempted to alter our society over time by physically infiltrating every aspect of our cultural environment.

1. In order to corrupt our _____ and, in so doing, _____ our lives. (page 7)

2. It has been Satan's intention since the beginning of man to inflict as much pain on God's elect and to take as many as possible with him into an eternity separated from God. (page 7)   True ____ False ____

3. We are all _____ and are subject to its vices, so it makes sense that we need guidelines in order to break free from the _____. (page 7)

We will be using the Bible as the ultimate resource and support for the theories and ideas contained within this book. For most then the question will be, "How were the scriptures written and how do we know if they are accurate?" Many acknowledge the Bible exists (kind of hard to deny), but they doubt the Bible's accuracy and would rather intellectualize creation based on their own beliefs or rationalize creation based on the theory of evolution.

Take a moment and write down your thoughts and beliefs about the accuracy of the bible. Be prepared to discuss. _____
_____
_____

4. The factual reality is this: the Bible was _____ by God to 40 writers and written over a period of _____. (page 7)

5. In 1947 Bedouin shepherds found the first of what we now know as the "_____ _____," which are ancient texts that have been authenticated by numerous scholars and archeologists. (page 9)

6. The people who penned the content of the Bible lived in different time periods and had no way of _____ with one another. (page 10)

Read Hebrews 4:12 (page 10)

7. "For the word of God is _____ and _____, and sharper than any ____ _____." (page 10)

8. We all are born into this_____, which is one of pain and suffering. However, there is another world that is free of pain and suffering, a world that is _____, but more _____ than the physical world we now live in. (page 12)

Have you ever cried out to God or to an unknown creator? Describe your experience. Be prepared to discuss. _____
_____
_____

9. Write the definition of the Trinity found on page 15. _____
_____
_____
_____

Read John 1:1-5 (page 16)

10. "In the beginning was the _____, and the _____ was with God, and the _____ was God." (page 16)

11. "In Him was _____, and the life was the _____ of men." (page 16)

12. "The light shines in the _____ and the darkness did not _____ it." (page 16)

13. We have the word today in the form of the _____. (page 16)

14. "Him" is Jesus Christ. (page 16)   True ____ False ____

15. The word comes _____ in our hearts through acceptance of the _____. (page 16)

26 • Freedom from S.I.N. Study Guide

16. John provides us with _____ so that we can come to a clear _____ of Jesus Christ and His connection to God and God's desire to _____. (page 16)

CLOSE IN PRAYER — Journal your prayer requests

Notes & Prayers: _____
_____
_____
_____

DAY TWO — Role of John the Baptist

Open in Prayer — Invite the presence of the Holy Spirit

1. John the Baptist, who was sent by God to _____ to the _____. (page 16)

Read John 1:6-13 (page 17)

2. John the Baptist is actually bearing witness to the three parts of the Trinity. Can you name them?

   _____
   _____
   _____

3. Finish this sentence. "But as many as received Him, to them He gave _____ _____." (page 17)

Read John 1:29-31 (page 17)

4. John the Baptist, baptizing people in the Jordan River, sees Jesus approaching and unknowingly gives those around him a glimpse of the future purpose Jesus was to play. To what purpose was John referring? (page 17)

   _____

5. John the Baptist left no doubt who Jesus was by his personal admission, "I have _____ and _____ that this is the _____." (page 18)

Read John 1:32-34 & Matthew 3:11 (page 18)

6. Is there more than one form of baptism? (page 18)   Yes ____ No ____

The Trinity • 27

7. How does John the Baptist define his baptism as compared to Jesus' baptism? John's was a baptism of _____ and Jesus Christ's was a baptism of the _____ and _____. (page 18)

Write your thoughts on the different methods of baptism mentioned in number seven. Be prepared to discus. (For those of you who have not been baptized and would like to be, please speak with your facilitator) _____
_____
_____
_____

Read John 10:25-30 (page 19 & 20)

8. Did Jesus claim to be God?   Yes ____ No ____

9. What declaration did Jesus make in verse 30? (page 20) _____

Read John 10:33 (page 20)

10. Many religions describe Jesus as a _____, a _____ or a _____. (page 20)

11. S.I.N.'s deception with this line of thinking is Jesus could not be a good anything if He was _____ about being _____. (page 20)

12. When we invite _____ into our hearts we in essence become one with _____, but we are not _____. (page 20)

Read John 1:14-15 (page 20 & 21)

13. John the Baptist bore witness to Jesus. Who was Jesus based on this scripture? _____

14. How could we ever know the _____ Christ endured at that point in time by taking on the sins of _____ past, present and future? (page 21)

15. Out of God's_____, He _____, granting us access into His eternal kingdom. (page 21)

Read Matthew 27:46 (page 21)

16. God through His _____, Jesus Christ, had become the _____. (page 22)

Read Isaiah 53:5 (page 22)

17. Whom was Isaiah referring to in 53:5? _____ (page 22)

Read Matthew 27:50 (page 22)

18. That was the day God bore our iniquity and defeated S.I.N. in the physical realm! (page 22)   True ____ False ____

CLOSE IN PRAYER — Journal your prayer requests

Notes & Prayers: _____
_____
_____
_____

DAY THREE — Attributes of God

Open in Prayer — Invite the presence of the Holy Spirit

1. What are the three divine personalities of God? He is _____, _____ and _____. (page 22 & 23)

Read Jeremiah 32:17-18, Psalm 139:7-12 & John 4:24 (page 22 & 23)

2. Define Omnipotent _____

3. Define Omnipresent _____

4. Define Omniscient _____

5. God the Son is all _____, but came to us in the _____ form by way of the _____. God the Holy Spirit is all _____ but intercedes through our _____ being, _____ our conscious minds. (page 23)

Read Philippians 2:6-7 & John 14:26 (page 23)

6. The CEO sets the _____, the President _____ and the team _____. God sets the vision for all creation, Christ assembles and leads the team and the Holy Spirit carries out the vision. (page 23 & 24)

Read Genesis 1:1-2 & Genesis 1:3-25 (page 24 & 25)

7. Did God consider His creation good or bad? _____

8. Now imagine for a moment if the universe were out of balance. What would our world look like? (page 25) _____
   _____

9. Can the created fully understand the creator? (page 26)   Yes ____ No ____

10. Where is God's universe factory? (page 26) _____

Write your thoughts about your answer to numbers nine and ten and be prepared to discuss. _____
_____
_____

11. God manifested Himself in the fleshly form through the man we know as Jesus Christ, and He did so in three parts: _____, _____ and _____. (page 27)

12. Has God's creation of man changed since He created Adam and Eve in the garden? (page 27)   Yes ____ No ____

Read 1 Thessalonians 5:23, Hebrews 13:5 & Job 32:8 (page 27)

13. We are not three separate beings, but one being. Like Jesus, we are _____, _____ and _____. (page 27)

14. John revealed to us that God the Son is the _____. Thus, God continues to dwell among us and is available to us by and through His _____, whether we choose to acknowledge His or not. (page 27)

15. God is longing to reveal His _____ in life. (page 28)

Read Exodus 3:14 (page 28)

16. God the "I AM" was relaying to Moses that He is _____ and _____. (page 28)

In John 8:58, Jesus previously had made the declaration, "Most assuredly, I say to you, before Abraham was, I AM." (page 20)

17. What does this say about Jesus and God? _____

CLOSE IN PRAYER — Journal your prayer requests

Notes & Prayers: _____
_____
_____
_____

DAY FOUR — **Holy Spirit and the infinite nature of God's creation**

Open in Prayer — Invite the presence of the Holy Spirit

1. God set the _____ and He came to earth through _____ in order to assemble the team, a team that consisted of _____ original members. (page 28 & 29)

Read Luke 6:13 (page 29)

2. God the _____ didn't speak on His own authority, but by the authority given to Him by God the _____. Jesus was God's _____. (page 29)

Read John 5:19 (page 29)

3. The Holy Spirit moved through them, _____ them to speak the Word with _____. (page 29)

Read Acts 4:31 & John 14:12 (page 29 & 30)

4. When we accept Jesus Christ He imparts His power to us so that we will do greater works. (page 29)   True ____ False ____

Read Galatians 4:1-7 (page 30)

5. "God has sent forth the _____ of His _____ into our _____." (page 30)

6. Through the birthing process, we in essence become _____ with God of our own _____. (page 30)

Read Revelation 3:20 & John 3:16 (page 31)

7. He stands knocking "at the door" to our hearts, longing to have fellowship with all who invite Him in. He longs to bless us with "everlasting life." It is the Holy Spirit knocking on our hearts door. (page 31)   True ____ False ____

The Trinity • 31

8. If God's Holy Spirit is infinite and we were created in God's image, what does that say about our spirit? (page 31) _____

Read Matthew 22:32 and Revelation 1:8 (page 31)

9. God is a God of the _____, not of the _____. (page 31)

10. How do you define the Alpha and the Omega? (page 31) _____

11. Our beginning was with God, because in Him and through Him _____ _____; we were made in His image, according to _____ _____. (page 32)

12. We were made into substance through birth and _____. (page 32)

Read Luke 16:19-25 and Matthew 10:28 (page 32 & 33)

13. Could these scriptures possibly support a theory that our physical man perishes, but our spiritual man lives for all eternity? (page 33)   Yes ___ No ___

14. How could an all-encompassing God of Love allow such a chasm or separation between the eternal realms of Heaven and Hell? (page 33) _____ _____

15. Free will says it is our decision to _____ God for who He is and who He says He is. (page 33)

16. When we choose not to have a fellowship with God and not to acknowledge His ultimate authority, then we like _____, _____ from God. (page 33)

Meditate on the following question. Does your spirit live on for all eternity? Be prepared to share your thoughts and opinions. _____ _____ _____

CLOSE IN PRAYER — Journal your prayer requests

Notes & Prayers: _____ _____ _____ _____

DAY FIVE—Ways we reject God and consequences for rejecting God

Open in Prayer—Invite the presence of the Holy Spirit

Read Hebrews 9:27 & Matthew 24:36 (pages 34)

1. God understands creation because _____ — from the beginning of time up to the time He takes us home for all eternity. (page 34)

2. When is the judgment? Before we die or after? _____ (page 34)

3. Christ's return is a time that no one knows. Why? (page 34) _____
   _____
   _____

4. For that reason, _____, so if anyone claims to know, you had better _____. (page 34)

5. Creation is not a _____ birthed by man or out of man's _____ of Christianity or any other _____, for that matter. (page 34)

6. God is eternal: _____. (page 34)

Read Hebrews 13:8-9 (page 34)

7. We are taking a big chance if we make the decision to reject God. Not only are we rejecting Him here on earth in our _____ form, we are also rejecting Him for all eternity in our _____ form. (page 34)

8. We are rejecting Him in three ways. First, we reject His _____, then we reject His _____ and lastly we reject His _____. (page 34)

9. An infinite God pauses within His creation to reach out to us in physical form in order for each one of us to join Him in His spiritual _____ — a _____ that has no boundaries, no has no limitations, no exclusions and is infinite in scope. (page 34)

10. What three things has God given to all who believe? His _____, His _____, and His _____. (page 34)

11. God is so _____, yet so _____, that the _____ human has a hard time understanding the _____ character of God. (page 34)

The Trinity • 33

12. Out of _____, many have and will continue to discount His awesome power and His truths and stand destined to live eternally separated from His awesome presence. (page 34)

Read Isaiah 14:12-14 & John 14:3, 6 (page 35)

13. Hell is a lonely place, and Satan's torment because of his separation from the Creator is still too much for him to bear alone. (page 35)   True ____ False ____

14. Jesus said to him, "I am the _____, the _____, and the _____. No one comes to the Father except through Me." (page 35)

Take a moment and write down your thoughts about your answer to question number 14 and be prepared to discuss. _____
_____
_____

CLOSE IN PRAYER

Summarize what the Lord showed you this week:

_____
_____
_____
_____
_____
_____
_____
_____
_____
_____

Week II
Satan's Intended Notion

Day One — Society Defined

Open in Prayer — Invite the presence of the Holy Spirit

From the beginning, mankind has been deceived. Out of our ignorance and naiveté, we have been led down a destructive path; a path we have continued to follow throughout generations, beginning with Adam.

Read Revelation 12:9, Luke 10:18 & John 10:10 (page 37)

1. It is time we understood and uncovered S.I.N. for what it really is, "Satan's Intended Notion," and we learn through his deceptive tactics that it has become "_____ _____." (page 37)

2. How has S.I.N. become "Societal in Nature?" _____

Take a moment and list some ways you have experienced spiritual erosion and societal erosion. What is the parallel between spiritual erosion and societal erosion?

3. How has he accomplished this? His intention is to accomplish this through the _____ of our _____ and by using men and women with _____. (page 37)

4. Write the definition of Society found on page 38. _____

Satan's Intended Notion • 35

5. "Climactic in nature" – is your life a series of _____ and _____?
   (page 38)

6. The valley is where the real _____ gets done, and if we are honest, it is where we spend the _____ of our lives. (page 39)

7. Are your relationships _____? Do you know what determines _____? (page 40)

8. Are we drawn to other people by mutual interest? (page 40)   Yes ____ No ____

9. Does it matter if those interests are healthy or not? (page 40)   Yes ____ No ____

Why are questions 8 & 9 important? _____
_____
_____

Take a moment and answer the following questions found on page 41:

What is the climate of your social circles? _____
_____

Are they healthy, loving and life building? _____

10. Do you believe that like attracts like? (page 41)   Yes ____ No ____

11. Do you believe people in general are followers or leaders? _____
    (page 41)

12. Do you think certain groups are concerned about _____,
    _____? (page 41)

CLOSE IN PRAYER – Journal your prayer requests

Notes & Prayers: _____
_____
_____
_____

DAY TWO – Gang Formation

Open in Prayer – Invite the presence of the Holy Spirit

1. One only has to study the psychology behind the principle theory of "_____ _____" to understand the _____ we are faced with in our current society. (page 42)

2. Write the definition of a Gang found on page 42. _____
   _____
   _____
   _____

3. List some reasons why people join a gang? (page 42) _____
   _____

4. "Gangs on the whole do not have good intentions, but are bent on some _____ behavior _____ to society." (page 43)

5. Name a few of the men in who have been able to influence whole societies with their personal agendas. (page 43 & 44) _____
   _____
   _____

6. Many become _____ of _____ in order to entice and lure additional members into their ranks. The goal is to assume power, and once in power, they _____ to preserve that power. (page 43)

7. Who are the most feared and ruthless in the gang population? (page 45) _____
   _____

8. Super predators are less likely to believe in _____, more likely to purport to be on _____ side. (page 45)

9. Out of spiritual ignorance, these men will most likely spend an _____ with Satan in the _____ as a _____ of the destruction they have brought on millions of people. (page 45)

Read Revelation 21:8 (page 46)

10. Yes, many good organizations have been formed based on the principle of "gang formation," we just don't refer to them as "_____." (page 46)

11. It is also extremely important to understand that the reason this _____ works is that it is based on a _____, a _____ that can be found in Ecclesiastes in the Bible. (page 46)

Satan's Intended Notion ▪ 37

Read Ecclesiastes 4:9-12 (page 46)

12. The reason this scripture is powerful, as we will learn in more detail later in the book, is because the "_____" is present in the Trinity: God the Father, God the Son and God the Holy Spirit. (page 46)

13. When building relationships, there is power spiritually. When we acknowledge and invite the _____ as the third cord, we invite the _____ to join in and bless the union. (page 46)

14. Since this principle is present in the _____, whether we choose to acknowledge it or not, it is effective when employed in the _____.

Write some ways you can invite the Holy Spirit to be the third cord in your life. Be prepared to discuss.

_____
_____

CLOSE IN PRAYER — Journal your prayer requests

Notes & Prayers: _____
_____
_____
_____

DAY THREE — True Intentions

Open in Prayer — Invite the presence of the Holy Spirit

1. What is the difference between the men and women who build entities that are healthy for society and the men and women who build entities to control society? (page 47) _____

2. The _____ of their heart will reveal the _____ contained therein. (page 47)

3. Should it come as any surprise that these terrorist of 911 were themselves "_____" by _____ and as a result, the whole world is still paying _____ for their _____ and _____? (page 47)

4. Governments will even debate the right or wrong issues based on their own cultural backgrounds before making a unified effort to combat the destructive behavior and guard against future terrorist attacks. (page 47 & 48)   Yes ____ No ____

38 • Freedom from S.I.N. Study Guide

Read the definition of Jihad and then Proverbs 26:21 (page 48)

5. These men and women appeal to the _____ and the _____, those easier influenced – the _____, not the leaders. (page 48)

6. Most importantly, they deceptively recruited them to give their lives for a _____ _____. (page 48)

7. Fidel Castro admittedly lied to everyone when he started talking about revolutionizing Cuba. (page 48)   True ____ False ____

8. Castro was successful in his quest because Cuba at the time lacked a _____ _____; the corrupt were taking advantage of the lack of _____ _____ to export Cuba's resources. (page 49)

9. Castro knew what to say, because he knew the _____. He also understood historically the change that could be brought about if he could get enough people _____ behind him. He rallied the support of _____ _____, the _____ being one. (page 50)

10. History has revealed that the true nature of his heart was never democratic, but self-serving: to take control and ultimately dominate. (page 50)   True ____ False ____

11. For the most part, people are well intended. However, a misguided intention can have an effect on a nation and ultimately the world. (page 51)   True ____ False ____

12. If those intentions are birthed out of a _____, anyone or anything that tries to thwart their effort will become their _____. (page 51)

13. Deception is as alive today as it has been since the beginning of time. (page 51) True ____ False ____

14. Thus, _____ personalities are able to _____ and _____ _____ personalities. (page 51)

15. For a group to be _____ there has to be a _____ and a _____ of action. (page 51)

16. The entities were _____, and their members had a _____ _____, however they were accepted and became part of a family. (page 51)

Write about a time in your life when someone with an ill-intended heart, has attempted to take advantage of you? Be prepared to discuss. _____
_____
_____
_____
_____

CLOSE IN PRAYER — Journal your prayer requests

Notes & Prayers: _____
_____
_____
_____

DAY FOUR — Jesus Christ

Open in Prayer — Invite the presence of the Holy Spirit

Read Matthew 1:21-23 & Isaiah 7:14 (page 51 & 52)

1. At the bottom of page 51, what is the leader's name? _____

2. Jesus Christ didn't have the _____ we have today or the _____ cited in our previous two examples. (page 52)

3. He chose a few very unassuming men to _____, _____ and ultimately _____ to carry out _____ _____ for all humanity. (page 52)

Read Luke 3:23 & Luke 4:16 — 21 (pages 52)

4. The people in his village were _____ and felt _____, because they knew him only as the son of Joseph and Mary, a common couple in the community. (page 52)

Read Luke 4:28 — 30 (page 53)

5. As a result of Jesus' declaration, what did all those in the synagogue intend to do with Him? (page 53) _____

Read Matthew 3: 1-7 (page 53)

6. They had no idea that John the Baptist was paving the way for Jesus, who was ready to begin His ministry and claim His _____. (page 53)

Read John 1:35-39 & John 1:40-53 (page 53 & 54)

7. How did Jesus assemble His team? (page 54)
   _____

Read Luke 23:2 (page 55)

8. At this time, the _____ started to become concerned, anxious and finally threatened, knowing that action needed to be taken for fear of a rebellion. (page 55)

9. Jesus was referring to Himself as a _____, a _____ that would ultimately rule a _____ for _____. (page 55)

10. They ignorantly assumed that He was declaring himself king in order to birth a movement, all part of a dangerous ploy to overthrow their political system.
    True ____ False ____

11. The hierarchy of that political system feared for their lives. (page 55) Why? _____

12. Those abuses existed to support the lavish lifestyle of the _____ _____ authorities. (page 55)

13. It wasn't until Jesus was joined by others that the movement became a threat to those leaders. (page 55)   True ____ False ____

14. Does the example of how Jesus birthed His ministry sound similar to the previous examples we have explored? (page 55)   Yes ____ No ____

CLOSE IN PRAYER — Journal your prayer requests

Notes & Prayers: _____
_____
_____
_____

Day Five — History

Open in Prayer — Invite the presence of the Holy Spirit

1. We showed in each of our examples that to the establishments in power, the movements seemed to be a threat to society. I ask you then, what was the difference? (page 56)
   _____

Read Matthew 12:34-35, 1 Corinthians 4:5, Proverbs 14:10-14 & Hebrews 10:22 (page 56)

2. History has proven that Christ had good intentions, and his intentions were birthed out of a _____. (page 56)

3. Christ's message of repentance and forgiveness of sin was guided by love. The only thing He asks us in return is that we love Him. (page 56)   True ____ False ____

Read Deuteronomy 6:5 (page 57)

4. We are all influenced by those around us, and stronger personalities have a way of dominating and setting the _____ of our society. (page 57)

5. Here in America, we have people of different cultural backgrounds from all over the world. These are in essence subcultures, but once they become citizens, they are asked to _____ into our _____ culture. (page 57)

6. Cultural groups may remain distinctively different, but once united into the overall culture, the common bond becomes our inalienable rights granted by our country. (page 57)   True ____ False ____

7. Our _____ understood firsthand that people were going to disagree about how the country should be organized and ultimately governed. (page 57)

8. They created three separate but unified branches of government: the _____, _____ and _____. (page 58)

9. Our forefathers didn't attempt to _____, _____ or _____ who we are at the core, but rather established a system whereby there would be checks and balances. (page 58)

10. Their intention was to _____ the nation from one person or one group's ideals that could, not held in check, _____ the core principles and beliefs the country was built on. (page 58)

42 • Freedom from S.I.N. Study Guide

Take a moment and list some spiritual principles our Founding Father's used to establish the foundation of our country. Be ready to discuss.

_____
_____

11. Our Founding Fathers were intent on preserving those _____, yet at the same time honoring the _____ of the people. (page 58)

12. We should thank our Founding Fathers for their _____ in creating a system of checks and balances. (page 58)

13. We study history as a reminder of times past. It helps us understand and not forget the reason our forefathers came to this country in the first place and why they laid the foundation on such solid ground. (page 58)   True ____ False ____

14. Oftentimes, our _____ are birthed out of our own upbringing and the abuses we have been subjected to from _____. (page 59)

15. It is not until we look back upon _____ that, as a whole, we realize the danger and the _____ wrought by individual ideals that have been _____ on the masses. (page 59)

16. Jesus came, experienced life with all its hardships and offered His _____, while _____ our _____. (page 59)

Read Colossians 1:15-20 (page 59)

17. Jesus Christ is "_____, _____" which is made up of His followers. (page 59)

Read 1 Peter 5:8 & 2 Corinthians 11:3 (page 60)

18. The devil is an _____ and has _____ our societal structures in order cause us to _____ by adhering to unbiblical doctrines. Doctrines which are fraught with lies from the men and women who sometimes knowingly and many times unknowingly, have joined his gang and declared war on _____. (page 60)

19. Furthermore, as a result of S.I.N., our nation as we know it today has become divided over numerous secular issues. (page 60)   True ____ False ____

Close in Prayer

Summarize what the Lord showed you this week:

_____
_____
_____
_____
_____
_____
_____
_____
_____
_____

WEEK III
THE SET-UP

DAY ONE — Satan's Role in History

Open in Prayer — Invite the presence of the Holy Spirit

Read the opening paragraph in Chapter 3 and answer the following questions.

Write down your thoughts on what kind of life are the children destined to have. Be prepared to discuss. _____
_____
_____

1. Wouldn't the pain of conviction be too great? (page 61)   Yes ____ No ____

2. Where does the enemy reside? (page 61) _____

3. We are born into this world in a society not of our choosing. (page 61)
   True ____ False ____

Read Isaiah 14:12 & 2 Corinthians 11:14 (page 62)

4. Lucifer was a created being that, by his God given nature, _____. (page 62)

5. Lucifer had a _____, and along with that _____, he also had a _____. (page 62)

Read Isaiah 14:13-14 (page 62)

6. It was Lucifer's _____ or _____ to _____ God and _____ His throne. (page 62)

7. Lucifer's _____ at the time was so strong and _____. We learn in scripture that _____ of the angels in heaven bought into his treason and ultimately were _____ with him for all eternity. (page 62)

Read Revelation 12:7-9 (pages 62 & 63)

8. Referred to as the "_____...called the _____." (page 63)

9. Satan's fall from grace was never God's _____, but as a result, became God's _____ of creating a climate of _____.

10. God didn't _____ for Lucifer to rebel any more than he _____ for us to rebel against Him today. It was Lucifer's _____, his _____ decision. (page 63)

11. Is it the nature of a loving God to _____ everyone to love Him _____? (page 63)

12. How could He love us _____ unless He gives us a _____ to love Him _____? (page 63)

13. His love is unconditional and offered _____ to any and all who _____ to accept it. (page 64)

14. When Satan was cast from Heaven, he was well aware of God's love, God's nature and God's plan for man. (page 64)   True ____ False ____

15. Satan, however, a _____, can only be in _____ _____. (page 64)

16. Having that knowledge, he knew he was going to have a _____.

Write your definition of the true meaning of unconditional love. Be prepared to discuss.

_____
_____
_____

CLOSE IN PRAYER — Journal your prayer requests

Notes & Prayers: _____
_____
_____
_____

DAY TWO — Satan's Role in History / Original Sin

Open in Prayer — Invite the presence of the Holy Spirit

Read Ezekiel 28:15 (page 64)

1. Why didn't God kill Satan and all of his rebellious angels? (page 64) _____
   _____

2. Satan, being an _____, had to live somewhere, just not in _____ with God. (page 65)

3. God in his _____ could not allow _____ to exist much less _____ in heaven, so when Satan _____, he and his followers were not only cast out of heaven, but became _____! (page 65)

4. Satan and his cronies would become the _____ by which each of God's creations would be able to exercise their free will. Either _____ God as their Father or to _____ God and live _____ from God for all _____ along with Satan. (page 65)

5. I challenge that it was for this reason that God cast him to _____ instead of relegating Satan to some far away planet. (page 65)

Read Genesis 1:26 & Genesis 1:27-28 (page 65 and 66)

6. Who did God grant dominion over all the earth? (page 66) _____

7. How frustrated do you think this made Satan? Very Much or Very Little (circle one)

8. Satan is not omnipresent, so he had to figure a way to _____ himself in order to _____ God's plan of creating a _____ garden where man could _____. (page 66)

9. Satan's set-up was to plant his _____ into the _____ of every human being through the natural _____. (page 66)

Read Romans 8:28 (page 66)

10. God is _____ and all things work _____ for good to those who love God. Thus supporting the claim that Satan would ultimately be _____ to allow all of _____ an opportunity to execute _____. (page 66)

The Set-Up • 47

11. God doesn't _____ in His _____ nature of creation that was set in _____ when he _____ the world into existence. (page 67)

Read Revelation 21: 6-8 (page 68)

12. What people are referred to in this verse? _____
_____

13. What does this verse say their eternal fate will be? "They shall have their part in the _____ which burns with _____, which is the _____." (page 68)

Read Genesis 1: 11 (page 68)

14. Here it is confirmed, "God said" so it is accurate to assume that in his position, _____ was listening as God spoke creation into existence. Thus, he most likely had _____ of God's plan to create the garden. (page 68)

15. Everything was good before Satan's _____. But evil was birthed as a result of Satan's _____ and sin was birthed after Satan's _____. (page 69)

16. God had not _____ for Satan to fall, but He was not going to be _____ His creation as a _____ of Satan's rebellion. (page 69)

Read Genesis 2: 19-20, Genesis 2:18 & Genesis 2: 21-23 (page 69)

17. God continued with His creation in spite of Satan's rebellion.   True ____ False ____

CLOSE IN PRAYER — Journal your prayer requests

Notes & Prayers: _____
_____
_____
_____

DAY THREE — Temptation of Man

Open in Prayer — Invite the presence of the Holy Spirit

Read Genesis 2:8-9 & Genesis 2:16-17 (pages 70)

1. God provided instruction to Adam in the garden, commanding him _____ from the tree of "_____." (page 70)

2. God did not give Adam a _____ and didn't feel the need to _____ His command. (page 70)

3. God _____ obedience. (page 70)

4. The tree represented a _____, a _____ that would determine the _____ of man's heart. The same _____ still exists today. (page 70 & 71)

5. Adam and Eve were obviously _____ around all of God's creation at the time, so the _____ posed no visible threat. (page 71)

6. Because of man's _____ nature Satan saw an opportunity to trick him into _____ against God. (page 72)

Read Genesis 3:1-5 (page 72)

7. Satan, the deceiver, _____ the truth to make evil sound _____. (page 72)

8. The evil he was _____ Eve with in this portion of scripture was _____ to God's command. (page 72)

9. Being _____ are no excuse for ignorance. (page 72)

10. S.I.N. always seeks a _____ and does so through _____. (page 72)

11. Whom did Satan deceive? (page 72) _____

Read Genesis 3:6 (page 73)

12. Where was Adam at the time of Satan's deception? (page 73) _____

13. Who was to blame for the fall of man? (page 73) _____

14. Adam did not exercise his _____, which was his God _____ right. (page 73)

Read James 1:15 (page 73)

The Set-Up • 49

15. Adam's _____ is still haunting us and ultimately opened the door for _____ in our relationships and promotes _____ in the societies in which we live. (page 74)

16. We all continue to eat from the "_____." (page 74)

Write some of the ways we are still eating from the "Tree of the knowledge of good and evil" and be prepared to discuss. _____
_____
_____

CLOSE IN PRAYER — Journal your prayer requests

Notes & Prayers: _____
_____
_____
_____

DAY FOUR — Forsaking Authority / Born into Sin / Separation from God

Open in Prayer — Invite the presence of the Holy Spirit

Read Ephesians 5:25 & Ephesians 5:33 (page 74)

1. God intended for Adam to exercise _____ in the garden and to _____ Eve, to _____ her, stand up, and be the _____ God created him to be. (page 74)

2. Has man's role in marriage changed since the days in the garden?
   Yes ____ No ____

3. Adam became Satan's _____ and would forever be known as the "_____ _____." (page 74)

4. Every time Adam and Eve _____ a child, S.I.N. would be _____ in the baby's _____. (page 74)

Read Psalm 51:5 (page 75)

5. Sin always results in guilt, cover up and eventually death — spiritual death! (page 75)   True ____ False ____

Read Genesis 3:7-19 & Genesis 3:22-24 (page 75 & 76)

6. Adam and Eve died to a _____ in a perfect place that was void of pain, suffering, war and destruction of any kind. (page 75)

Read Genesis 4:1-2 (page 77)

7. After God declared His judgment on Adam and Eve for their rebellion, we learn in scripture that Adam "_____," or had intercourse with Eve. (page 76)

8. She bore him _____, who became the first sons the world had ever known. (page 76)

Read Genesis 4:3-4 (page 77)

9. In this portion of scripture, Eve's sons brought an offering to God. Was it cold of God to look down on Cain's offering? (page 77)   Yes ____ No ____

10. God knew the _____ of the givers. (page 77)

11. Cain showed that his _____ was _____ by not giving the first fruits of his produce. (page 77)

Read Genesis 4:6-10 (page 77)

12. Cain did not choose to _____ God's _____, _____ himself and get back on track. (page 77)

13. Instead of heeding God's advice, what did Cain do? (page 77) _____

14. "Sin lies at the door. And its desire is for you, but you should rule over it." Is this scripture still valid today? (page 77)   Yes ____ No ____

15. What cried out to God after Cain murdered Abel? (page 78) _____

Read Genesis 4:11-15 (page 78)

16. Cain's separation came as a _____ of his sinful _____. (page 78)

17. Our blood too will _____ and our _____ too will live on after our natural body has gone back to dust. (page 78)

18. Will your spirit reside somewhere for all eternity? (page 78)   Yes ____ No ____

The Set-Up • 51

19. It is either heaven and eternity in _____ with God or hell and eternity _____ from God. (page 78)

Read Revelation 1:18 (page 79)

20. Death, we have shown, is _____ and ultimately brings _____ from God. (page 79)

CLOSE IN PRAYER — Journal your prayer requests

Notes & Prayers: _____
_____
_____
_____

DAY FIVE — Dysfunction of the Family

Open in Prayer — Invite the presence of the Holy Spirit

1. S.I.N. has an effect on our society as a whole and taints the family structure. (page 79)
   True ____ False ____

2. Sin brings _____, _____, _____. (page 79)

3. The very first family was _____ and our families today are still _____! (page 79)

How could we really know what determines functional if society sets the functional and dysfunctional standard? Write your answer to the following question and be prepared to discuss. _____
_____
_____

4. Inherent in every human being there is a God-given ability to discern right from wrong, good from evil. (page 79)   True ____ False ____

Read Mark 4:15 (page 79)

5. Satan's plan is to _____ our thinking, so that we become _____ by what our _____ nature tells us. (page 79)

Read Proverbs 1:8, Proverbs 6:20 & Ephesians 6:1 (page 80)

6. We are specifically instructed to obey the father's _____
   and the mother's _____. (page 80)

7. Is there a spiritual blessing for the children when the parents impart spiritual wisdom to their children?   Yes ____ No ____

After World War II, many women were left to raise the children and manage the affairs of the home. As a result, many men failed to fulfill their role in the home, resulting in the mothers providing not only the law, but also the instruction.

Write about your childhood experience. Did your Mother and Father follow Proverbs 1:8 in your family? Be prepared to discuss. _____
_____
_____

8. With the absence of the Father to support the teaching/law and no adequate command/instruction, there was no balance in the home. This resulted in a generation that was not properly instructed according to _____. (page 81)

9. In today's society, we are classified by how we are raised, where we were raised and the socio-economic level attained. Societal levels determine your place, like it or not. (page 81)   True ____ False ____

10. Since God is good and out of His goodness, He will not _____, Satan is able to create _____ on earth. He plants evil thoughts intended to _____ even the strongest and most well-meaning individuals into thinking, "If God is good, why allow all this destruction?" (page 81)

Read Romans 5:12 (page 82)

11. We are all _____ until the day we die, but we are also _____ _____ until the day we die. (page 82)

12. Christ loves us and wants us to spend _____ with Him, and Satan despises us and wants us to spend an _____ from God. (page 82)

13. Sin takes its root in our heart in the form of Satan's seed; that seed_____ _____, and then begins to _____ in our lives. (page 82)

14. From a standpoint of revelation, we need to see S.I.N. for what it is: a _____ force created by Satan to _____, hold us back, disqualify us and, ultimately, _____. (page 82)

15. Why not wake up and acknowledge the fact that he is trying to _____ _____ by the way he has so molded our _____? (page 83)

Read Romans 5:19–21 & 1 John 2:16 (page 83 & 84)

16. S.I.N. is _____, which leads to _____, because it causes us to separate from God. (page 83)

17. When we give in to "the lust of the flesh, the lust of the eyes, and the pride of life," we are just tops spinning in Satan's playroom and all the while he is just _____ _____, _____ and ultimately _____ into eternal separation from God. (page 83)

CLOSE IN PRAYER

Summarize what the Lord showed you this week:

_____
_____
_____
_____
_____
_____
_____
_____
_____
_____

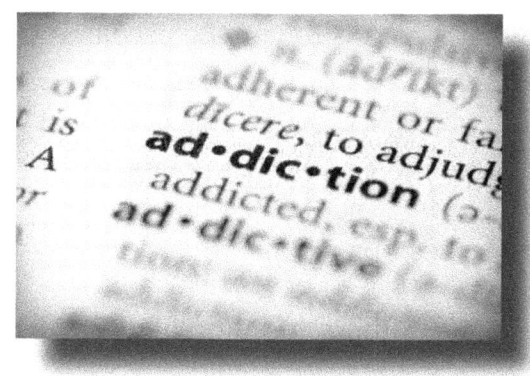

WEEK IV
SOCIETAL ADDICTION

DAY ONE – The Addictive Process

Open in Prayer – Invite the presence of the Holy Spirit

Today, we have unknowingly become addicted in our societal upbringing in the same way some become addicted to a substance. The sad truth is we are glorifying Satan on a daily basis through the decisions we make.

1. Satan has been molding _____ since the beginning of man's tenure here on earth. He has set the _____ for how people within those societies should live. (page 85)

Read John 14:1-2 (page 85)

2. Satan wants to confuse us with the lure of _____. (page 85)

3. God wants us to know that He understands that we need certain material possessions, but those possessions are not to take the place of our _____ with Him. (page 85)

Read Matthew 6: 31-34 (page 85 & 86)

4. God intends for us to keep a _____ and _____ by entering into a right relationship with Him. As a result, He will _____ in ways we can't imagine. (page 86)

5. The true "American Dream" is really about the _____ God has given us to worship as we please, to _____ in accordance with free will. As a result, realize the _____ He provides everyone in His creation. (page 86)

Write your definition of the "American Dream," and what it means to you. Be prepared to discuss. _____
_____
_____

6. Society teaches the _____ of what God teaches. (page 86)

7. Deception causes us to _____ ourselves, _____ others and ultimately _____ our Creator. (page 86)

8. Summarize and list the key points in the definition of Addiction found on page 87.
_____
_____

9. Our lives are patterned by the world around us. (page 87) True ____ False ____

10. This world is: things we are _____ as we grow up, the things we are _____ with by our peers; and the things we _____ our system. (page 87)

11. Name a few forms addiction comes in. (page 87) _____
_____

Read Jeremiah 17:9-10 (page 87)

12. Everyone in our world today has some form of addiction. (page 87)
    True ____ False ____

Write some ways we have become addicted to our surroundings. Be prepared to discuss.
_____
_____
_____

13. We have been _____ and in effect _____ by our Surroundings and the _____ that is so prevalent today. (page 87)

14. What is meant by the concept "trash in — trash out"? (page 87) _____
_____

15. The trash that comes in _____ with the trash that is _____ _____ and when the two collide, there is real trouble. (page 88)

Read Mark 7:14-23 (page 88)

16. We have deceived ourselves into thinking that we can entertain the lusts of this world and at any time "_____," and that somehow we are in control. (page 88)

17. We might not get to enjoy the _____ of S.I.N. if this revelation occurs. (page 88)

CLOSE IN PRAYER — Journal your prayer requests

Notes & Prayers: _____
_____
_____
_____

DAY TWO — Roots of Addiction

Open in Prayer — Invite the presence of the Holy Spirit

1. There are _____ of these addictions. (page 88)

2. Cite some ways those roots become manifested. (page 88) _____
_____

3. The addictions themselves are not the real problem. (page 88)   True ____ False ____

4. The real problem is found in the _____ of those manifestations — some of which go deep into our _____. (page 88 & 89)

5. Cite some examples where those roots can stem from. (page 89) _____
_____
_____

Take a moment and list any roots that you believe are still active in your life. Be prepared to discuss. _____
_____
_____

6. Because of the _____ of our hearts, we react, manifesting _____ as we grow and mature. (page 89)

7. We have more external influences on us today because of the media than at any time in the history of man. (page 89)   True ____ False ____

Societal Addiction • 57

8. Wrong choices _____ the roots of our addictions. (page 89)

9. The root of Eve's addiction was her _____ of God's word and was _____ when she ate of the apple. Adam became addicted by _____ of the same. (page 89)

10. Wars are being waged daily all over the world. Where are some of the places wars are being waged? (page 89) _____
_____

11. The true enemy does not care how the battle is fought or where the battle is waged, only that the battle is waged and _____. (page 89)

12. S.I.N., _____, which is happening all around us—his intended notion—has permeated our society. (page 90)

Read the story on page 90

13. Addiction was rooted in _____ not in his control, but events nonetheless; he had to deal with in his life. (page 90)

14. Drinking soon became a way for him to escape his _____ and falsely gave him a sense of _____ over his emotions. (page 90)

15. The story on page 90 is primarily about alcohol addiction. Is alcohol a drug? (page 91)
Yes ____ No ____

16. Do the painkillers in the medicine cabinet of most American homes qualify as a drug? (page 91)   Yes ____ No ____

17. They are all _____ substances and when abused will at some point take control of one's life. (page 91)

18. S.I.N. knows that _____ will keep you in the cycle of your chosen addiction! It keeps the _____ of those addictions hidden. (page 91)

CLOSE IN PRAYER — Journal your prayer requests

Notes & Prayers: _____
_____
_____
_____

58 • Freedom from S.I.N. Study Guide

Day Three — Cycle of Addiction

Open in Prayer — Invite the presence of the Holy Spirit

1. One could argue that the cycle of addiction begins by way of introduction. (page 91)
   True ____ False ____

2. Society has taught us through advertising that drinking is an integral part of _____ and something to _____. (page 91)

3. We know that not everyone _____ at the same rate, so just because someone turns 21 overnight doesn't mean they are going to _____ or that _____ won't lead to more serious issues. (page 91)

4. They rarely have the proper _____ knowledge of the _____ dangers of alcohol. (page 92)

Read Genesis 19:32 (page 92)

5. The amount of any drug we start consuming depends not on our level of education, but on the level of our _____ and the _____ in our life.

6. Everyone has the same self—control and everyone is experiencing the same issues in life. (page 92)   True ____ False ____

Read the story at the bottom of page 92

7. This young man had been set up by his behavior prior to that night. What did it cost him? What did it cost the person he hit? (page 92)
   _____ / _____

8. He was deceived by an enemy, and in this case, the enemy disguised itself in the form of a _____. (page 92)

9. The _____ because the effects of the substance eventually wear off, at which point one is faced with their issues. As with any _____ _____ substance, the only way to avoid facing the issues of life is to keep abusing the substance. (page 93)

10. We don't intend to become addicted or intend for the substance to adversely affect our lives. (page 93)   True ____ False ____

11. Has alcohol or any other mind—altering substance had a positive influence on your life? (page 93)   Yes ____ No ____

12. Would you agree that parents could do a much better job parenting if alcohol or other substances were not present in the home? (page 94)   Yes ____ No ____

13. The enemy has used _____ alone to kill more people than cancer and to bring more _____ than all other issues among families. (page 94)

14. One glass of wine, one beer or one drink is not destructive, and the people that exercise that kind of self-control are not bound by the substance. (page 95)
True ____ False ____

15. When we become more _____ by the effects of the wine more than the wine itself, we become _____ by the _____ behind the wine. (page 95)

16. The people who will take offense to my stance on this subject are the ones who are in _____. They would not be content to debate the possibility that they have a problem, because doing so would _____ their ignorance and could threaten their _____. (page 95)

17. Satan himself has _____ them and is in _____ of their lives. (page 95)

Read Proverbs 20:1 (page 95)

18. Societal addictions are real, and we can't escape their effects. They are deeply rooted in our culture and hidden away in our hearts because of past hurts and pains. (page 95)   True ____ False ____

CLOSE IN PRAYER — Journal your prayer requests

Notes & Prayers: _____
_____
_____
_____

DAY FOUR — Addictive Erosion

Open in Prayer — Invite the presence of the Holy Spirit

1. Steeped in our _____, we have become ignorant of what I call the _____ that has been wrought on our society throughout time. (page 95)

2. We have been _____ to the point where now, if someone came up and asked us to fill our tank, we would be suspicious and think, "Does this vagrant want a handout?" (page 95)

3. What are two of the biggest and most obvious areas we have seen addictive erosion at work? (page 96) _____

List some other areas where you see addictive erosion occurring in our society. Be prepared to discuss. _____
_____
_____

4. Our _____ system has become lax to the point where we consider nudity on the screen as a _____ medium to be enjoyed. (page 96)

5. We don't see it as a _____ that could possibly be used as a tool of the enemy to lead us astray from proper _____ and _____ behavior. (page 96)

6. We don't associate this content with the erosion of our _____, a contributor to _____ diseases. (page 96)

7. Our younger generations are being weaned and in time will have _____ _____ of our past system of moral decency. (page 96)

8. The ethical and moral decline in our society has been a slowly _____ _____ and all the while has _____ us into thinking that these mediums are good. (page 97)

9. For many, they feel a sense of entitlement; that no one has a right to _____, everyone should be able to make his or her own decision about what is _____ _____, _____. (page 97)

10. Everyone has a choice or the option to act a certain way or to look at certain content, but not at the _____ of others and the _____ as a whole—especially the _____ that will one day be the ruling class of our society. (page 97)

Societal Addiction • 61

CLOSE IN PRAYER — Journal your prayer requests
Notes & Prayers: _____
_____
_____
_____

DAY FIVE — Freedom from Addiction

Open in Prayer — Invite the presence of the Holy Spirit

1. God provides the tools necessary to overcome these addictions and live free from the sinful nature of our heart. (page 97)   True ____ False ____

2. The only way to be delivered from an addictive lifestyle is through the _____ _____ of Jesus Christ and _____ to His word. (page 97)

3. Satan's reign of terror, though still evident in the _____, has been defeated in the _____. (page 97)

Read Luke 10:19-20 (page 97)

4. We have been so clothed in our _____, so trained by society and so deceived by Satan that we have rested on ignorance in our _____ of God's power. (page 97 & 98)

Read Job 38:1-41 & Isaiah 40:21-22 (pages 98 & 99)

5. God hasn't changed in the time that has elapsed since Job was alive, and He isn't going to change after you and I pass from this earth. (page 99)   True ____ False ____

6. So whose story of creation are you going to believe: some _____ _____ living in modern times, or the _____ speaking through a Job or an Isaiah living in ancient times before Christ was born? (page 100)

Read Joshua 24:14-15 & 2 Peter 3:8 (page 100)

7. God created everything we _____ have knowledge of in six of His days, and in doing so, formed the world through _____ in order for the whole of mankind to have purpose. (page 100)

8. Are His six days like yours and mine? (page 100)   Yes ____ No ____

9. Stan longed to be God, so he used his own _____ in his _____ of man. (page 100)

10. Knowing what you know about _____, do you really want _____ to define creation for you? (page 101)

Read Genesis 2:7 & Ecclesiastes 12:7 (page 101)

11. Where did we come from and to what will we return? (page 101) _____

12. Where does our spirit go? (page 101) _____

13. God longs to bring us into His kingdom, so much so that He came to us in the _____ _____. (page 102)

14. Ignorance is like a _____, _____ that can shield the mighty flames of the sun, can snuff out the moon and can bring _____ upon our lives. (page 102)

15. Those clouds shroud the _____ in our life regardless of how many books we have read, how many lectures and seminars we have attended, or how many debates we enter into. (page 102)

16. We need to wake up to the fact that _____ has so clouded our vision that we don't know who God really is, and we have become content to live lifestyles set in the _____. (page 102)

Read Jeremiah 1:4-5 & Matthew 26:26-28 (page 102 & 103)

17. Even when we take a leap of faith and God comes through, we continue to _____ _____. (page 103)

18. Freedom from _____ is accomplished once we accept the _____ into our hearts. (page 103 & 104)

Read Proverbs 16:9 (page 104)

19. Why don't we see _____ for who he really is and see that he has used _____ to distort our thinking, dampen our faith and question God's intentions? (page 104)

20. God wants to direct your path toward an eternity with Him. (page 104)
    True ____ False ____

Write your thoughts on 2 Peter 3:8 and be ready to discuss. "But, beloved, do not forget this one thing, that with the Lord one day is as a thousand years, and a thousand years as one day." _____
_____
_____
_____
_____

CLOSE IN PRAYER

Summarize what the Lord showed you this week:
_____
_____
_____
_____
_____
_____
_____
_____
_____
_____
_____

WEEK V
PLAYING LIFE

DAY ONE — Running with the Herd / Pick and Choose to Suit

Open in Prayer — Invite the presence of the Holy Spirit

We are all just playing a game and that game is called "Life." Every day is a new day, a new adventure, and we tread on in anticipation.

1. We _____ move through life, hoping that one day we will awaken to find that our lives had _____. (page 105)

2. There is a tendency to _____ of scripture that line up with our lifestyle instead of _____ God's Word in order to _____ sin in our lives. (page 105)

Read the story under "Running with the Herd" on page 105 & 106

3. The enemy, Satan, wants us to _____ his behavior, not God's behavior. S.I.N. will always lead us astray, and if the enemy can command the _____ of the leaders, it will be easy to command the of _____ the followers. (page 106)

Read Proverbs 20:18, Proverbs 21:5 & Proverbs 21:11 (page 106)

4. In all aspects of life, we have a _____ to go along with what _____ else is doing. (page 106)

5. We listen to the same _____, view the same _____ and _____ _____ by the society in which we have become immersed. (page 107)

Meditate on the following questions and be prepared to discuss.

Playing Life • 65

- Are we simply weak and feel a need to follow something or someone, regardless of his or her intentions?
- Are we exhausted to the point where we are just going along to get along?
- Are we preparing for the mission we were put here on earth to achieve?
- Have we become prey to complacency, where we run the risk or have a tendency to choose counsel that provides the easiest route in life, even if we sense it is the wrong route?

_____
_____
_____
_____

6. The reality is this: God is in control, and no matter what route we take in life, if He is truly in our hearts, all routes will ultimately lead back to Him. (page 107)
   True ____ False ____

7. It's usually not until we take a _____ and see ourselves as God sees us that we can _____ our emotions and actions in time for God to _____ into His beauty of creation. (page 107)

8. Like the mustang, God is still looking down on us, pleased with His creation. Don't you think it is time to let go of our own _____ and give in to God's pursuit? (page 107)

9. We take the _____ out of context and wonder why we are so _____ in today's society. (page 107)

Read 1 John 2:1, Romans 7:17 & Romans 6:1 (page 108)

10. Once you trust in Christ there will be _____ of sin, and if you truly made a _____, you should follow the Word of God. Not _____ it to justify your sinful nature. (page 108)

11. When we continue our _____ and hold out to our peers that it is _____ in God's eyes, are we not _____ by the enemy? (page 108)

12. If we choose to remain in _____ sin, we are being _____. (page 108)

Read Matthew 7:13-14 & Proverbs 16:25 (page 109)

13. Narrow is the _____ and difficult is the way which leads to _____, and there are _____ who find it.

Read Deuteronomy 22:21 & John 8:3-11 (page 109 & 110)

14. In the previous scriptures, does it appear that the women were guilty of sin and the elders justified in imposing punishment?   Yes ____ No ____

15. What was Jesus' response in the story found in John? (page 110) _____
_____

16. Jesus didn't say you can _____, go to the priest, make _____ and all will be _____. (page 110)

17. Jesus was _____ her that once forgiven, all you have to do is _____, and you won't have to deal with the issue ever again. (page 110)

CLOSE IN PRAYER — Journal your prayer requests

Notes & Prayers: _____
_____
_____
_____

DAY TWO — Pick and Choose to Suit (continued)

Open in Prayer — Invite the presence of the Holy Spirit

Read over the 613 "Mitzvos" or Mosaic law found in the appendix of the book. (page 259)

1. Is the law negated just because we cannot or do not adhere to the law? (page 110)
   Yes ____ No ____

2. Our prisons are filled with men and women who claim their _____, but regardless are still _____ for their crime. (page 110)

3. We do not _____ of God, but through _____, we are offered _____, allowing us to fully know His love for us. (page 110)

Read Romans 5:18-21 (page 111)

4. In this scripture we read, "But where sin _____, grace _____ much more." The remainder of the verse states, "So that as sin reigned in death, even so grace might reign through righteousness to _____ _____." (page 111)

5. Scripture is to be taken in totality and read with an _____ toward God's _____ love. (page 111)

Read Isaiah 53:1-12 & Jeremiah 31:31-34 (page 111 & 112)

6. The Old Testament prophecies found in Isaiah and Jeremiah have been fulfilled by the Lord's coming. (page 111)   True ____ False ____

7. The Bible is flowing back and forth from the Old Testament to the New Testament clearly in support of itself. (page 113)   True ____ False ____

8. What are we possibly risking when we miss-interpret scripture and try to convince others we are correct? (page 113) _____

Read 1 Corinthians 6:9-10 & 1 Corinthians 6:18-20 (page 113)

9. The above scriptures cover just about every kind of _____ imaginable. (page 113)

10. We can avoid putting ourselves _____ eternally by checking what anyone says against the _____. Even if what we are hearing is being _____ through a fellow child of God or from the pulpit of our church. (page 113)

11. When we stand before God all we have to say is, "But, Lord so-and-so told me this behavior was okay, I didn't know you warned us about it in the scriptures." (page 113 & 114)   True ____ False ____

12. If there is an area of sin in your life that God has _____ to be wrong through scripture you need to heed His warning. But if you are _____ _____ by claiming God's grace to justify the _____ and _____ in that act of sin, you are _____ under Satan's or S.I.N.'s influence. (page 114)

13. How will you know if a specific behavior is sinful? (page 114) _____ _____

Read Matthew 7:1-3 (page 114)

68 • Freedom from S.I.N. Study Guide

14. It is in His power to _____ us for our sin, in His power to _____ us of our our sin. He alone executes judgment and determines our _____ fate. (page 114)

15. We must look at the Bible in _____ and not just _____ scripture to suit a need or to mount a defense for intellectual debate. (page 114)

16. Scripture will not always _____ to us, but just because we become confused or even deceived by someone's opinion or interpretation of scripture, it _____ God's love for us. (page 114)

17. He will bring _____ into the hearts of those who have rightfully chosen to accept His free gift of salvation. There will be mountains of consequence to circle until a _____ is made to receive conviction by revelation, confess our sin, repent and _____ . (page 114 & 115)

18. We think that by _____ God's Word to fit our behavior we will be free from God's _____ . When in reality we have become slaves to sin and are already being held in judgment. (page 115)

CLOSE IN PRAYER — Journal your prayer requests

Notes & Prayers: _____
_____
_____
_____

DAY THREE — To Pull or To Push / Satan's Playbook

Open in Prayer — Invite the presence of the Holy Spirit

1. We need to know how the _____ in order to defend those _____ . Once we identify the enemy's methods, we have a choice: use _____ or use _____ . (page 115)

2. Why _____ when you could _____ ? (page 115)

Read the stories on page 115 & 116

3. Is our natural response always the correct or best response? (page 116)
   Yes ____ No ____

4. Life's _____ can have much the same effect on us. They can be so powerful that we become overwhelmed by their _____ over us. (page 116)

Playing Life • 69

5. When we resist the urge to do what is comfortable and we put our training to work, we can overcome life's struggles. (page 116)   True ____ False ____

6. Instead of fearing our circumstances or struggles and _____, we should _____ and _____ with the Lord's power. (page 117)

7. When we _____ by pressing in and giving our fear of the unknown to Him, He will _____ us. (page 117)

Read Proverbs 1:7 (page 117)

8. We know that in life for any team to be successful, they must have a _____ _____ made up of _____, and then they must _____. (page 117)

9. What if we could turn the tables and peek into Satan's playbook? (page 117 & 118)
_____

10. The enemy only has three primary weapons. What are they _____, _____, & _____. (page 118)

11. All his other weapons are _____ that stem from these three. (page 118)

12. We are all too familiar with the enemy's first play, temptation, which is usually brought about in the _____. (page 118)

13. Temptation will come to us all, but our _____ to it is under our _____. (page 118)

14. The power is within us, but first we have to _____ that we can overcome. Then we have to _____. (page 118)

Read Genesis 4:6-7 (page 118)

15. What was God's instruction to Cain about sin? (page 118) _____

Read Exodus 16:1 and Exodus 20:1-2 (page 118 & 119)

16. What is the name of the mountain where the Lord gave Moses the Ten commandments? (page 118) _____

17. What is the name of the nearby wilderness? (page 118) _____

Read Exodus 20:3-17 (page 119 & 120)

18. List the Ten Commandments and be prepared to recite.
   1) _____
   2) _____
   _____
   3) _____
   _____
   4) _____
   5) _____
   _____
   6) _____
   7) _____
   8) _____
   9) _____
   10) _____
   _____

CLOSE IN PRAYER — Journal your prayer requests

Notes & Prayers: _____
_____
_____
_____

DAY FOUR — Satan's Playbook

Open in Prayer — Invite the presence of the Holy Spirit

Read Luke 10: 18-19 & Romans 8:11 (page 120)

1. Satan does not want us following the Lord's _____ that enable us to draw upon the power available to us through the _____. (page 120)

Meditate on the following questions and be prepared to discuss:

- Have you ever been drawn to something you knew in your heart to be wrong?
- Have you been drawn in to an area of sin innocently, only to linger long enough that later you felt further enticed to explore that area of sin in more depth?

- Where did it lead you?

_____
_____
_____
_____
_____

Read I John 3:5 then read about the Temptation of Christ found in Matthew 4:1-11 on pages 121-123

2. God knew that it is only through _____ that one can truly understand what happens to man and woman when sin comes knocking on the door of their hearts. (page 121)

3. God's grace carries us in our times of physical weakness by strengthening us in spirit. (page 121)   True ____ False ____

Read 2 Corinthians 12: 9-10 (page 121)

4. The only way to thwart the enemy's attacks is through _____. The Word is _____, and when spoken, brings us _____ to overcome the obstacles that temptation tries to get us to stumble over. (page 122)

Read Matthew 26: 40 – 41 & James 1:12 (page 123 & 124)

5. We can give into temptation, or we can avoid temptation. The choice is ours because of the _____ granted by our Creator. (page 124)

6. What is the reward for the man or woman that overcomes temptation? _____ _____ (page 124)

7. The enemy's second play is _____ and is usually carried out in a more _____ way, by attacking our _____. (page 124)

Read Matthew 27:11-14 (page 124)

8. What was Jesus' response to Pilate? (page 124) _____

9. Satan's play of accusation always attempts to get us to _____, because there appears to be a _____ in what he is saying. (124)

10. When anyone brings a _____ accusation against you, do not _____ yourself. (page 124)

11. If we are truly innocent, God will mount a defense on our behalf. (page 125)
    True ____ False ____

12. S.I.N. doesn't care about the _____ of an issue, it only cares about keeping us _____ until eventually we want to_____ _____ and _____. (page 126)

Read John 8:32 & James 1:2-4 (page 127)

13. Through these scriptures, the Lord encourages us to embrace truth and faith. (page 127)   True ____ False ____

14. The third play the enemy deploys is _____, which is usually carried out in the form of a _____ attack. (page 127)

15. Satan will allow the _____ to be told, but will _____ a small enough _____ so the _____ will be under suspicion. (page 127)

16. The enemy wants to _____ us in his play of deception in order for those around us to _____ from us. (page 128)

17. Deception can be very subtle and to the general public may not even look like deception at all. (page 128)   True ____ False ____

Read Matthew 5:38-39, 2 Corinthians 11:3 & Hebrews 3:12-14 (page 128 & 129)

18. Don't trade your _____ for sin because sin is very _____! (page 129)

19. We need to study _____ so we will be able to speak it at the appropriate Time. Thus, guard against _____ the enemy in his game or _____ our actions in hopes that others won't see us through Satan's lies. (page 129)

20. If we allow our _____ to react, he will gain a lot of yardage on us. But, if we will _____—our line if you will—we stop Satan dead in his evil tracks! (129)

CLOSE IN PRAYER—Journal your prayer requests

Notes & Prayers: _____
_____
_____
_____

Playing Life • 73

DAY FIVE — The Armor of God

Open in Prayer — Invite the presence of the Holy Spirit

1. In the spiritual game of life, it would make sense to don the _____ _____ as we prepare our defense in order to _____ every aspect of our being. (page 129)

Read Ephesians 6:10-17 (page 130)

2. We gird our waist with the _____. Meaning that we must speak the_____ _____. (page 130)

3. Put on the breastplate of _____. Meaning we are to _____ _____ from the influences of the world. (page 130)

4. We shod our feet with the preparation of the _____. Meaning that we consciously acknowledge _____ as we walk along the paths of life. (page 130)

5. We grasp the shield of _____ that enables us to ward off _____ the enemy throws at us. (page 130)

6. We put on the helmet of _____ with full assurance of our _____ _____ . We then take up the sword of the _____, which is the _____ _____. (page 130)

Read Ephesians 6:18 & Isaiah 55:8 (page 130 & 131)

7. What are two very important aspects to understand about wearing the spiritual armor of God? (page 131) _____
_____

8. When you grasp this biblical concept, the difference is this: when the attacks come, they only lead you _____ into more of a _____ with the Father. (page 131)

Look back on your life and see if you can identify how the enemy has attacked you with his three primary plays: temptation, accusation & deception. Be prepared to discuss.
_____
_____
_____
_____

9. The enemy attacks us through _____, sometimes through our own _____, _____ and even the _____. He attacks through our _____ and life's _____. (page 132)

10. S.I.N. is _____ at your doorstep, and its _____ is for you! His _____ is to lure you into his trap, the trap of _____. (page 132)

Read John 8:44 (page 132)

11. In John 8:44 there are two terms used to describe the enemy, what are they? _____ & _____

12. Our struggle is with a _____ that has _____ _____ only, and that is to take us with him into eternal damnation! (page 133)

13. He attacks our core in an attempt to destroy us _____ — to destroy our _____ so that we will give up all _____. (page 133)

Read 2 Chronicles 20:17, Romans 12:19 & Hebrews 10:31 (page 133)

14. Who desires to fight the spiritual battles on our behalf? (page 133) _____

15. When we grasp this _____ and place it over us, as the armor in Ephesians 6, there is a _____ that none of us can quantify in the physical. (page 133)

Read the story on page 134

16. What is the ultimate reality of sin? It _____ us to its evil by getting us to _____ what we know in our _____, ultimately _____. Which is the very _____ of our relationship with God. (page 135)

Read Genesis 3:7-8 & Deuteronomy 32:39 (page 135 & 136)

17. God desires that you know the purpose for which He created you. (page 135) True ____ False ____

18. Satan will try to attack you on several fronts to keep you from _____ that purpose or coming to the _____ of the God-ordained purpose which He placed in your heart. (page 135)

Playing Life • 75

19. Isn't it time we don't defend against or engage an enemy who has no intention of resolution and does not care about right or wrong?   Yes ____ No ____

CLOSE IN PRAYER

Summarize what the Lord showed you this week:

_____
_____
_____
_____
_____
_____
_____

Week VI
Climactic Deliverance

Day One — Quick Fix

Open in Prayer — Invite the presence of the Holy Spirit

Wouldn't you love to be able to remove yourself from negative situations, deliver yourself from pain and suffering, free yourself from the sin that surrounds you and, in doing do, instantly transform your life?

1. Climactic deliverance is available to us all, but it is not a quick fix to our problems. In order for deliverance to be effective long-term, it takes time and discipline on our part. (page 137)   True _____ False _____

2. We have developed into a society that is climactic in nature — it seeks quick fixes and has bought into the _____. (page 137 & 138)

3. Even though there is an element of comfort stemming from our _____ _____, when we lose our balance — _____ — all that seems good is really leading us down a _____ toward death. (page 138)

4. God provides a way for us to be climactically delivered for all eternity. (page 138) True _____ False _____

5. Satan's desire is to _____ of climactic deliverance by creating a smoke screen so we can't see the _____ behind the concept. (page 138)

6. "If I had more money, I could live a better life and be happier." (page 139) True _____ False _____

7. In reality, it can and will bring _____ when gained hastily — when money is just given to us without being _____. (page 139)

Read Proverbs 20:21 (page 139)

Climactic Deliverance • 77

8. Does this scripture mean that everyone that wins something or receives a gift necessarily squanders it or brings destruction upon himself or herself? (page 139)
   _____

9. We have slowly been enticed by our _____ into thinking we need bigger and better places to live, bigger and better cars to drive and that somehow we _____ a better lifestyle. Without paying much of a price to get it. (page 140)

Read the last two paragraphs and the first two paragraphs on pages 140 & 141

10. What possible scenario is this loving and well-meaning father setting his daughter up for in life? (page 141) _____
    _____

11. S.I.N. will always distort our _____ when we are _____ to its schemes. (page 141)

12. Hopefully, this father taught his daughter that _____ tough times with her husband, _____ at all costs, would help to build a _____ . The type of _____ that later in life will _____ their marriage and _____ them closer together. (page 141)

13. When we lavish gifts on our children without the proper education, we can't always be sure what the ultimate outcome will be. (page 141)   True ___ False ___

14. We should encourage our children to rely on God for their ultimate supply. (page 141) True ____ False ____

15. Girls long for a _____ and when they have _____ that love, they grow up with a sense of _____. (page 141)

16. Young men who have been _____ and grow up knowing the _____ of hard work will experience a sense of _____ _____. (page 141 & 142)

Read Luke 15:11-13 (page 142)

17. S.I.N. will always tempt us into thinking we are _____; that there is something _____, _____, awaiting us. (page 143)

18. Sometimes in S.I.N.'s _____, we are drawn away from the _____ protection and covering that our families provide. (page 143)

CLOSE IN PRAYER — Journal your prayer requests

Notes & Prayers: _____
_____
_____
_____

DAY TWO — Entitlement

Open in Prayer — Invite the presence of the Holy Spirit

Read Proverbs 10:2 (page 144)

1. If Satan can _____ by integrating himself deeply into our society in such a way that we buy into his schemes, using his lies to _____, then he doesn't care about _____. He will have already accomplished his _____. (page 144 & 145)

Read Luke 15:24 (page 145)

Have you taken an inventory lately of your life where you might possibly be turning away from God the Father? Take a moment in prayer and ask the Lord to reveal any areas of your life that you need to turn back over to Him. _____
_____
_____

2. Today, many kids would rather sit in front of a flat-screen television playing video games than go outside. Much less explore opportunities that will help them grow and possibly put some money in their pocket. (page 145)
   True ____ False ____

3. The liberal lie of entitlement states: (page 145) _____
_____
_____

4. We are on the verge of breeding a whole generation that finds their reality wrapped up in the liberal lie of entitlement. (page 145)   True ____ False ____

5. What were some of the advancements that resulted from WW II? (page 146)
_____

6. The enemy's _____, unknown to us at the time, had moved us into thinking that _____, that we must drive the latest cars and live in the biggest houses. (page 146)

Climactic Deliverance • 79

7. What were some of the destructive results that came out of the Vietnam War? (page 147)
   _____

8. What came out of that generation? (page 147) _____

9. The liberal mindset that says, "Take from the _____.
   After all, everyone deserves to live a comfortable and luxurious life! We know what is best for you." (page 147)

10. The men and women that emerged from the Vietnam era have been deceived by S.I.N. into thinking that the same _____ that deceived them by telling them the Vietnam War was not political can _____ their healthcare, _____ their children and _____ for them in their old age. (page 148)

11. The truth is all men are _____ and should have the _____. The lie is all men _____ without having to _____ for it. (page 148)

12. Satan is a spiritual being and has always used current times to spin his tale of _____. (page 148)

13. One only has to look at the USSR to see how a whole nation crumbled as a result of this _____ governing system. Millions of people struggled lived in poverty and were denied the _____ that the system proposed to offer. (page 148)

14. As Christians, we are expected to go to _____, say our _____ and _____. We are to ask God for those things we are _____ and to provide for our _____ needs. How many of us really _____ so God can answer those prayers? (page 148)

Write your thoughts about the quote by Phillips Brooks on page 149. How it still applicable today? Be ready to discuss. _____
_____
_____

15. If your _____ in life is that you should be successful because those who have gone before you were successful, then the enemy has already _____ for spiritual _____. (page 149)

CLOSE IN PRAYER — Journal your prayer requests

Notes & Prayers: _____
_____
_____
_____

DAY THREE — **The Truth about Deliverance / True Deliverance**

Open in Prayer — Invite the presence of the Holy Spirit

Read 1 John 2:15-17 (page 150)

1. Because of the sinful nature of our hearts, we entertain _____, _____ and _____ to _____ the pain we so long to be free of. (page 150)

2. The reality is this: anything that is going to have _____ on your life will take time to acquire and will involve a process over time. (page 150)

3. When someone tells you that you can be "delivered," they are stating a _____. However, when they do so by telling you that the deliverance comes without any _____ on your part, they are _____ the serpent used to _____ Eve in the garden. (page 151)

4. In life, these _____ will sometimes bring you _____ _____ from your past; however, they are usually just _____ fixes for your _____ issues. (page 151)

Read Colossians 1:12-14 (page 151)

5. In this verse, from whom did God deliver us? (page 151) _____

6. Once you have been delivered, you can still enjoy the substance of your addiction. (page 152)   True ____ False ____

Read 1 Corinthians 3:9 & 2 Corinthians 6:1 (page 152)

7. However, because we are embracing a liberal way of thinking that deliverance is automatic and without any effort on our part, _____ easily creeps in (page 152)

8. We all need deliverance from the enemy. (page 152)   True ____ False ____

Climactic Deliverance • 81

9. It seems to make spiritual sense for God to immediately remove _____ of our character and all the _____ that have caused manifestations to occur in our life. Those that have caused so much destruction—some of which we are still paying _____ for. (page 152)

10. What I am conveying in this writing is that a deliverance which is really just a _____ _____ —one where you don't have to put any _____ so to speak; one that you really don't have to mix any _____ with; one that you don't have to _____ any Lordship in; is not a deliverance at all. (page 152)

11. What does the enemy do? He lies in wait for the _____ where he can pounce and reintroduce his _____ on you. (page 153)

12. Then you begin to doubt all that you thought you had been delivered from. (page 153) True _____ False _____

13. When it rears its ugly head, S.I.N. wants to use it to destroy your _____ _____ in God's Word. (page 153)

Read 1 Peter 5:8 (page 153)

14. "What are you going to do when the enemy pounces and tries to devour your soul?" (page 153) _____

15. What are you going to do when the issues of life rear their ugly heads once again? (page 153) _____

CLOSE IN PRAYER—Journal your prayer requests

Notes & Prayers: _____
_____
_____
_____

DAY FOUR—True Deliverance

Open in Prayer—Invite the presence of the Holy Spirit

1. True deliverance happens the day you _____ and become "_____." (page 153)

Read John 3:1-3 (page 153) & John 3:4-10 (page 154 & 155)

82 • Freedom from S.I.N. Study Guide

2. Jesus instructs Nicodemus twice in his eternal reality. First in John 3:3, "Most assuredly, I say to you, unless one is _____, he cannot see the kingdom of God." Again in John 3:5, "Most assuredly, I say to you, unless one is _____ _____, he cannot enter the kingdom of God". (page 153 & 154)

3. The Lord is always knocking at the door to _____ in hope that we will _____ of truth. (page 155)

4. We too, like Nicodemus, sometimes come to the Lord hiding from the world in order to ask our questions. (page 155)   True ____ False ____

Read Luke 17:20-21 (page 156)

5. I challenge that many in church today claiming to be _____ don't know what it means to be spiritually "_____." (page 156)

If you died and went to Heaven and the Lord just happened to be standing at the gate the very moment of your arrival and asked, "Son/Daughter why should I let you in?' What would your answer be?" _____
_____
_____
_____

6. Will being good grant you access to eternal life in Heaven? (page 156)
   Yes ____ No ____

Read Luke 18:18–19, Proverbs 20:6 & Psalm 103:12 (page 157)

7. You will be "_____" for all eternity. (page 157)

8. The Lord will remove the _____ and make a deposit in your heart of His _____, a deposit no one and nothing is able to steal. It will bring about your _____ in the spiritual realm and _____ your eternal course. (page 157)

Read Jeremiah 17:10, 1 Corinthians 2:10-12 & Proverbs 17:3 (page 158)

9. The answer to true deliverance is found in the heart of every believer. There is a response that we _____ and an _____ we must take. There will be _____ involved. (page 158)

Read John 5:24 & Romans 10:9-10 (page 159)

Climactic Deliverance • 83

10. In the following sentence fill in the blanks with the two primary requisites indicating you have eternal salvation. That if you _____ the Lord Jesus and _____ that God has raised Him from the dead, you will be saved. (page 159)

If you have not made a personal decision to accept Jesus Christ as your Lord and Savior, I want to encourage you to do so. Please read the scriptures and information on page 159 and if you feel led in your heart to trust in Jesus Christ why not get on your knees before God and pray the prayer on that page right now. Set your spiritual compass!

Maybe you have already prayed that prayer, but feel led to renew your commitment to the Lordship of Jesus Christ. Now is a good time to go to your knees, re-acknowledge Him as your Lord and Savior, and agree to serve Him the rest of your life. Reset your spiritual compass!

11. All babies are formed in the Mother's womb. When a baby is born, where does it emerge? (page 160) _____

12. In life we have been in our culture's womb for years, developing _____ and a _____. (page 160)

13. What happens as we emerge from the waters of baptism and what happens as a result of our washing away of the sinful nature? (page 160)
_____

If you have been baptized, take a moment and write down your baptism experience. How does it compare with John's method of baptism? Be ready to discuss. _____
_____
_____

Read Proverbs 11:30a, 1 Peter 2:21-25 & Matthew 5:14-16 (page 160 & 161)

14. Upon acceptance of His _____ and His _____ flowing through you, your light will also pour out on those around you, to the _____. (page 160)

15. You may not feel like your _____ the world. But one thing is for sure, when the God of the Universe by His spirit comes _____, you can't help but _____. (page 160 & 161)

Read Luke 22:70 (page 161)

16. When we embrace the Bible, the Holy Scriptures, as our point of reference, this literature testifies _____. (page 161)

17. "Climactic Deliverance" is available all right, because deep down inside we all want to be delivered from the grip of evil. The truth, void of all lies, is that when you accept the Lord Jesus Christ, you are delivered and it is climactic in the sense that you only do it once. (page 161) True ____ False ____

Read Hebrews 10:26-29 (page 162)

18. What warning does this verse give to the person who claims to be "Born Again," but continues in willful sin? (page 162)
    _____

Read Galatians 3:10-12 (page 162)

19. What instruction does this verse provide to all believers? _____
    _____

CLOSE IN PRAYER — Journal your prayer requests

Notes & Prayers: _____
_____
_____
_____

DAY FIVE — Four Keys to the Kingdom

Open in Prayer — Invite the presence of the Holy Spirit

1. What are four crucial keys to help you unlock your mind and soul in order to receive ongoing spiritual revelation from the Lord?
   1) _____
   2) _____
   3) _____
   4) _____

Read 1 John 4:1-3 (page 163)

2. Why do we want to share the good news of our belief in Jesus Christ? (page 163)
   _____
   _____

3. Invite them to _____, ask them for _____ and hear their _____ so that you can be encouraged to _____.
(page 163)

Read Psalm 119:11 (page 163)

4. Why do we want to read the Word? (page 163) _____

5. How do we hide the Word of God in our hearts? (page 163) _____

6. Why do we hide the Word of God in our hearts? (page 163) _____
_____

Read Hebrews 10:25 (page 164)

7. If you are looking for a Church, turn to God in prayer and He will guide you to a church that is _____, where the _____ is felt, where the _____ of _____ is evident. (page 164)

8. What instruction do we receive from this verse in Hebrews? (page 164)
_____

Please Note: We are not suggesting you change churches if you are currently a member of a church that believes the bible is the final authority. However, if you are already joined to a church body we would encourage you to embrace their teaching and begin to feed others with the eternal truths being taught.

9. Based on this verse in Hebrews what should we receive when we join with other believers? (page 164) _____

10. If God is going to be first in your life and you are going to live for Him, doesn't it make sense that you should _____ and _____ with Him? (page 165)

11. Why should it be a priority to spend time with God? (page 165) _____
_____
_____

12. You need to spend time with Him in the morning to _____ _____ for the day's events. You also need to spend time with Him at night to _____ of the day and ask _____ for a good night's sleep. (page 165)

13. What are some various ways to prime your spiritual pump in the morning? (page 165)
_____
_____

Write down when and how you spend your quiet time with the Lord. Be prepared to discuss. _____
_____
_____

14. Every Day is a new day and a new _____ to accept Him, trust Him, believe in him and walk with him. (page 166)

15. Deliverance is _____ and is walked out on a _____ basis. (page 166)

16. Repentance is nothing more than obedience to stay the course and keep you pointed in the right direction. (page 166)　　True ____ False ____

CLOSE IN PRAYER

Summarize what the Lord showed you this week:
_____
_____
_____
_____
_____
_____
_____
_____
_____
_____

Week VII
Stairway to Heaven

Day One — Acknowledgement and Acceptance

Open in Prayer — Invite the presence of the Holy Spirit

Our journey in life is like a stairway. We come out of the womb and whether we like it or not, we start climbing life's stairway.

Read 2 Corinthians 6:18 & 1 Peter 1:3-4 (page 167)

1. Why do we scale God's Stairway? (page 167) _____

Read Proverbs 15:24 (page 168)

2. What are the two eternal options based on this scripture? (page 168) _____
   _____, _____

Do you remember going to the mall as a child and riding the escalators? Did you ever try to go the opposite direction on the escalators? Have you ever tried running down an up escalator? Be prepared to discuss. _____
_____
_____

3. Our spiritual journey is a lot like riding an escalator. Once we make a _____ decision to accept Christ we climb aboard His "_____," well aware of our decision and where His stairway was leading. (page 168)

4. However, often times in life we are _____ going the _____, sometimes running away from God. (page 168)

Stairway To Heaven • 89

5. What are some of the primary steps on God's Stairway? (page 168 &169)
   1) _____
   2) _____
   3) _____
   4) _____
   5) _____

The Apostle Paul scaled these primary steps on God's Stairway. Luke gives an account of Paul's Damascus Road experience in Acts chapter 9:1-19. In Acts chapter 22:1-21 Luke relates Paul's personal testimony of the event before the people in Jerusalem.

Take a moment and read about Paul's experience found on pages 169-174

6. There can be no _____ without first _____ that God exists and learning who God is. (page 174)

7. Only through _____ can we have a _____ experience. (page 174)

8. Without this first step, we are lost in our sin and deceived. (page 175)
   True ____ False ____

9. The _____ in our society — regardless of our surroundings or the size of our toys — is that most of us are _____, pretending to be happy. (page 175)

Reflect back and write down a time in your life where you were practicing the same behavior in life, expecting a different result. Be ready to discuss. _____
_____
_____

10. Many people in our society rarely — if ever — _____ and others are what we call "_____," meaning they only attend church at _____. (page 175)

Read Revelation 3:15-17 (page 175)

11. What is God attempting to teach us in this portion of scripture? (page 175) _____
_____

12. What are some examples of S.I.N. listed on page 175? _____
_____
_____

13. Sin, once _____ has a toehold in our life and _____ in various ways. (page 175)

Read Proverbs 13:20 (page 176)

14. What do we risk by failing to acknowledge our sin? (page 176) _____ _____

Read John 14:6 (page 176)

15. Is there any other way to gain access to heaven other than through Jesus Christ? Yes ____ No ____

Read Revelation 21:27 (page 176)

16. Based on this scripture in what book do you want your name to appear? _____ _____. (page 176)

17. After our _____ has taken place, we begin to understand who _____ and what His love for us _____ _____. (page 176)

18. Can a person make a false decision to accept Christ in hopes of hedging his or her spiritual bets? (page 177)   Yes ____ No ____

Read Romans 10:9-10 (page 177)

19. Yes, once you make a heartfelt decision to trust in Jesus Christ, you have stepped on the Lord's _____ and are on your way to _____. (page 177)

Read John 10:29-30 (page 177)

20. God's escalator never breaks down. Can anyone take you off the escalator once you have made a heart decision to live for Christ? (page 177)   Yes ____ No ____

CLOSE IN PRAYER — Journal your prayer requests

Notes & Prayers: _____
_____
_____
_____

Day Two — Conversion and Brokenness

Open in Prayer — Invite the presence of the Holy Spirit

1. The conversion process usually begins with some catalytic moment or event, causing us to discover that our lives are heading in the wrong direction or spiraling out of control. (page 177)   True ____ False ____

2. We make a _____ effort to change. Through _____, we come to realize we are _____ to effect change in our life and give into God's _____ submitting to His Lordship. (page 177)

3. An interesting thing happens as we take the second step: areas of our life become _____; certain behaviors are _____; and the _____ _____sets in. (page 177)

4. However, in time, as we experience brokenness, we come to realize there is a _____ in Christ that brings lasting peace. We come to an _____ that our life has _____ meaning. (page 178)

Reflect back and write down a time in your life when you cried out for help, maybe asking the Lord to come to your rescue. Can you remember His response to your call? Be prepared to discuss. _____

5. God is patient, longing to reveal that He has been by your side all along, even in the midst of your _____. (page 178)

6. We are all born into sin. Therefore, we all must experience conversion and brokenness if we wish to scale God's stairway. (page 178)   True ____ False ____

Read Romans 5:12 (page 178)

7. If you are indeed on His stairway to heaven, you will sense _____ in the areas of your heart where you are not lined up with His will. If you don't deal with those areas, eventually you will experience the _____. (page 179)

Read Hebrews 13:5 (page 179)

8. Will God ever leave you or forsake you. (page 179)   Yes ____ No ____

9. He no longer sees your sin, but loves you _____ and will always bring you around to the right way of thinking. Yes, it might take _____. But make no mistake about it, God will _____. (page 179)

10. If you don't feel the pain of your sin then you need to re-evaluate your commitment to the Lord by asking, "_____?" (page 179)

Read Philippians 2:12 (page 179 & 180)

11. Whose responsibility is it to work out your salvation? (page 179) _____

Read Luke 16:14-15 (page 180)

12. It is extremely important to understand the difference between _____ _____. (page 180)

Read Romans 8:1 & John 16:8 (page 180)

13. Oftentimes, we might not even understand where the conviction is coming from or why we feel convicted, but somewhere _____, we know our behavior is _____. (page 180)

14. Some of us will suffer more _____ than others due to the _____ _____ that have been extracted from our societal upbringing prior to that point in time. (page 181)

15. What begins to happen when we surrender to the Lord and embrace His teaching? (page 181) _____
_____

Read Proverbs 1:7 (page 182)

16. Based on this scripture what do fools despise? (page 182) _____
_____

17. God longs to reveal your sin through _____ in order to free you. But it is up to you to take action, _____. (page 183)

18. What are some of the ways society has provided for us to medicate our pain? (page 183) _____
_____

Read 2 Timothy 3:1-7 (page 183)

19. Can you see any of the warnings outlined in 2 Timothy in today's world?
    Yes ____ No ____

Make a list of some of the ways you see Timothy's warnings present in your surroundings. Be ready to discuss. _____
_____
_____

Read John 3:18-19 (page 184)

20. We are talking about eternal life or eternal death. What does John suggest we do? (page 184) _____

CLOSE IN PRAYER — Journal your prayer requests

Notes & Prayers: _____
_____
_____
_____

DAY THREE — Restoration and Repentance

Open in Prayer — Invite the presence of the Holy Spirit

1. S.I.N. will attempt to _____ into its clutches by _____ us of our past behaviors and circumstances. (page 184)

Read Matthew 13:3-10 & Matthew 13:18-23 (page 184 & 185)

2. The key is to remain in _____, so that the _____ will prevail in our hearts. (page 185)

3. What does Godly sorrow through conviction calls us to? (page 185) _____

Read 1 Peter 1:23 (page 186)

4. What are the properties of an incorruptible seed? _____, _____, _____

In Matthew 16:18 Jesus tells Peter, "And I also say to you that you are Peter, and on this rock I will build my church, and the gates of Hades shall not prevail against it." Of course, this is the same Peter who denied Christ three times and forsook Him at His greatest hour.

94 • Freedom from S.I.N. Study Guide

5. Aren't we a lot like Peter, in the sense that we turn away when we are faced with difficult circumstances and feel abandoned by the Lord?   Yes ____ No ____

6. Have you ever _____ for something, only to be left holding your head in your hands thinking that your prayer has _____ _____? (page 186)

7. Have you ever thought, "Maybe I have _____? After all, if Christ is _____, why would He allow me to be _____ by my enemy?" (page 186)

Take a moment and list a time where you have struggled with God's answer or seeming lack of an answer to your prayers. Be prepared to discuss. _____
_____
_____

Read John 18:1-3, John 18:10-11 & John 21:14-19 (page 186 & 187)

8. Don't you think Peter was thinking these same thoughts?   Yes ____ No ____

9. After all, he had walked faithfully with Christ for _____ only to arrive in the garden of Gethsemane to witness _____. (page 186)

10. Peter was perplexed, to say the least, and was probably thinking, "This can't happen to my savior who has come to assume the _____ _____!" (page 186)

11. We are just like Peter in the sense that _____, we are _____. (page 187)

12. Isn't it interesting that just as Peter denied Christ _____, Christ restores Peter _____? (page 187)

13. It is only by our _____ that we experience the same godly sorrow Peter felt that leads us to repentance. (page 187)

14. It was always Christ's intention to _____ His Father had given Him by _____. (page 187)

15. And it was always God's intention to bring _____ through _____ _____ for all mankind. (page 187)

16. God loves us as sons and daughters. (page 187)   True ____ False ____

Stairway To Heaven • 95

CLOSE IN PRAYER — Journal your prayer requests

Notes & Prayers: _____
_____
_____
_____

DAY FOUR — Purification and Eternal Salvation

Open in Prayer — Invite the presence of the Holy Spirit

1. Purification is the ongoing process of _____ until the day we draw our last breath and realize the _____ promised by Christ. (page 188)

2. No matter how fast we try to run on God's stairway, we don't reach heaven any sooner. (page 188)   True ____ False ____

3. Over time, we become more aware of the _____ that caused our _____. Even though we have been delivered from that sin, there is _____ that needs to be stripped. (page 188)

4. The Lord _____, strips down our hearts through the process of conviction and then continually restores us until one day we will assume new bodies made in His image. (page 188)

Read John 17:19 (page 188)

5. When we are confronted with the various areas in our lives that need to be stripped, we should be _____, _____ in our response. Jesus was! (page 188)

Read Mark 10:15 (page 188)

6. Why do you think Jesus told his disciples that in order to enter the Kingdom, we must become like little children? (page 188) _____

7. Jesus understood how God created us. He also understood clearly how we become tainted by S.I.N. as we grow up _____. (page 188 & 189)

8. _____ are planted as we grow and age that one day will have to be extracted in order for us to live a productive life. (page 189)

9. We start taking on the _____. (page 189)

10. One would hope that before death comes that we would reach the truth—that all of our _____ was in vain. (page 189)

11. Our Lord longs to have _____ with us, if we would only lay down our _____ and our _____. (page 189)

12. By becoming his spiritual children and by His loving grace, we too will grow in _____, _____. (page 189)

Read 2 Peter 3:18 (page 189)

13. The Kingdom of God can only be realized through faith. (page 189)
    True ____ False ____

Read Romans 8:29 (page 190)

14. The Lord purifies us by rebuilding our lives in such a way that, over time, we take on more and more of _____, being conformed to the _____ _____. (page 190)

CLOSE IN PRAYER — Journal your prayer requests

Notes & Prayers: _____
_____
_____
_____

DAY FIVE — Ministry

Open in Prayer — Invite the presence of the Holy Spirit

Read Matthew 28:18-21 (page 190)

1. Name the three steps of ministry Jesus refers to in this scripture.
    1) _____
    2) _____
    3) _____

2. What is the name given for this scripture? (page 190) _____

Stairway To Heaven • 97

3. People can only be washed by the _____ and renewed by a _____ of the Trinity. (page 190)

Read 2 Timothy 2:2 (page 191)

4. He has imparted His unseen power that is _____ here on earth. It is a spiritual power that, once _____, understood and exercised, allows us to move the spiritual mountains surrounding us. (page 191)

Read Romans 10:13-15 (page 192)

5. There is an incredible feeling — an _____ — that comes from _____ _____. (page 192)

6. What is a simple yet effective prayer that will keep your life from ever becoming spiritually boring? (page 192)
   "_____"

7. The Father of creation has molded you into His glorious image for one purpose and one purpose only, _____. (page 192)

Read John 17:16-18 (page 192)

8. Everyone born to this earthly existence has a _____ to fulfill. (page 192)

Read Ephesians 4:11-14 (page 193)

9. Christ desire is that we would be fully equipped for "the _____, for the edifying of the body of Christ!" (page 193)

10. He wants us all to come to "the _____ of the faith and of the _____ of the Son of God." (page 193)

11. He does not want us to be "_____" by every doctrine of man. (page 193)

12. If they are not true representatives of God, then folks, we have put ourselves at risk. (page 193)   True ____ False ____

Read Matthew 12:34 (page 194)

13. We don't need anyone to intercede on our behalf with God. (page 194)
    True ____ False ____

14. We need our Church and ministers to aid us in identifying our _____ and confirm that what we are hearing is in fact from _____. (page 194)

Read 1 Corinthians 12:12, 18, James 1:17 & 1 Corinthians 12:20-21 (page 194 & 195)

15. If you find joy in your chosen profession, it is because something you are doing is lining up with your _____. (page 194)

16. When the Holy Spirit shows up in our lives, we _____, but we _____. Therefore, we enter the kingdom of God _____. (page 195)

Read Hebrews 11:1-3 (page 195)

17. Now that we have entered into a spiritual realm that is not visible to our eyes, we are _____ bound by our sin and death _____ has a hold on us. In fact, death only _____ us to a new life; a life of _____ in Christ's Kingdom. (page 195)

18. The Lord wants us to embrace the fact that once we step on His escalator, we step into the _____. (page 195)

Read Revelation 21:4, Revelation 21:10-21 & Luke 23:42-43 (page 196 & 197)

19. No matter which stairway we are on, we still have to deal with life's struggles and hardships. (page 197)   True ____ False ____

20. God's stairway leads to a wonderful place void of _____ a place Jesus called _____. (page 197)

List some ways you are involved in the work of ministry. List some ways you could be more involved in the work of ministry. Be prepared to discuss. _____
_____
_____
_____
_____
_____
_____

CLOSE IN PRAYER

Summarize what the Lord showed you this week:

Stairway To Heaven • 99

WEEK VIII
PRACTICE ROUNDS

DAY ONE — Biblical Practice Rounds

Open in Prayer — Invite the presence of the Holy Spirit

Before beginning today's lesson please read the note on page 199 & 200. After all, isn't it how we finish the game we call life that is important?

1. Tiger Woods stood on the number one tee box at _____ for the first time and must have been thinking that he had finally arrived. (page 199)

2. He didn't just show up the day of the tournament and decide he was going to play in the Masters. (page 199)   True ____ False ____

3. Our life experiences are a series of _____, and if we don't embrace them and utilize them along our journey, they become wasted. (page 200)

4. Tiger's journey started when he was just _____ to his father and could _____ swing a golf club. For the next _____ he prepared for the day that he would compete for the green jacket and the right to say, "I came, and I conquered Augusta." (page 200)

5. Now let's be real, we all know that the best and most well-meaning preparation still doesn't ensure _____. (page 200)

6. Those practice rounds have a name. They are called _____. (page 200)

Practice Rounds • 101

7. Our practice rounds become our _____ along the way. If we embrace them, not only will they propel us on our journey, but we will be able to use them as _____. We use them to help _____ others on their journey through life. (page 200)

Read Corinthians 9:24-25 (page 200 & 201)

8. The difference in our preparation for the final and ultimate spiritual tournament is this: we all have a chance to win, and our reward is "_____." (page 201)

9. That crown of righteousness is _____, _____ with God the Father, Son and Holy Spirit. (page 201)

10. "Why would our practice for the _____ be any different than the Practice Tiger and the other professional golfers employ in their quest for the coveted green jacket?" The _____ is much bigger than the Masters. (page 201)

11. One day we will all stand before the Creator in hopes that your life has counted. (page 201)   True ____ False ____

Read Matthew 25:21 (page 201)

12. We will all be held _____ for how we prepare for the tournament of life. (page 201)

Read 1 Peter 4:17 (page 201)

13. In life, we will play many _____ throughout the years in _____ to stand on that sacred tee box in order to vie for the coveted prize. (page 202)

14. However, as we read in Matthew 7:14, "Because _____ and difficult is the way which _____, and there are few who find it," some will win, but some will lose. (page 202)

Read John 14:24 (page 202)

15. The Lord has given us a _____, _____ _____ if you will, that helps us compete for the prize. Compete in such a way that all who follow the rules and stay in the game will ultimately win the prize. (page 202)

16. When we learn to embrace those practice rounds, we gain _____ and life becomes much more _____. (page 202)

CLOSE IN PRAYER — Journal your prayer requests

Notes & Prayers: _____
_____
_____
_____

DAY TWO — Life of Joseph

Open in Prayer — Invite the presence of the Holy Spirit

We are going to take the next two days and look at the life of Joseph. His story is an incredible biblical example of the importance practice rounds play in our lives.

1. Joseph's _____ were actually _____ _____ preparing him to fulfill God's purpose for his life. (page 203)

Read Genesis 37:2-4 & Genesis 37:5-11 (page 203)

2. Joseph has two dreams, which he shares with his family, and as a result, his brothers become _____, and Jacob, his father, _____ him. (page 203)

3. Joseph's brothers had about all they could take from this arrogant and prideful 17-year old. What did they decided was the best course of action to eliminate any threat he might have for their father's affection. (page 204) _____

Read Genesis 37: 21-22 (page 204)

4. Reuben's plan was to _____ into putting Joseph _____ so that he could return later, retrieve Joseph, and take him back home to his father. (page 204)

5. Was Reuben's plan successful? (page 204)   Yes ___ No ___

Read Genesis 37: 26-27 (page 204)

6. The brothers _____ Joseph to Ishmaelites, who transported him to _____ with the intention of selling him for a profit. (page 204)

7. The brothers dip Joseph's tunic in _____, then send it to Jacob. (page 204)

Practice Rounds • 103

Genesis 37: 29-33 & Genesis 39:1-6 (page 204 & 205)

8. The Ishmaelites had traveled to Egypt and upon their arrival in Egypt sold Joseph to _____, a captain of the guard in Pharaoh's army. (page 205)

9. The Lord's hand was on Joseph, "he was a successful man." What did Potiphar do as a result of the Lord's blessing on Joseph's life? (page 205) _____
_____

Read Genesis 39:1-10, Genesis 39:19-20 (page 206)

10. Potiphar's wife immediately brought an _____ against Joseph and _____ to her husband, saying that Joseph had been the one trying to take advantage of her. (page 206)

11. Potiphar, obviously upset, has Joseph thrown into _____. (page 206)

Read Genesis 39:23 (page 206)

12. We learn that in prison, the Lord's Hand continued to be on him and after a period of time, he was _____ of all the other prisoners. (page 206)

13. In these scriptures, we see that in prison, Joseph was tending to two of the King's men, a _____. Each had a _____ and Joseph was able to interpret their _____. (page 206)

Read Genesis 40:1-8 & Genesis 40:9-23 (page 207 &208)

14. After interpreting the butler's dream, Joseph made a _____, asking that he remember him when he went before Pharaoh. Joseph knew the butler would be the only one of the two alive to make the appeal before the King. (page 207)

15. Does the butler keep his commitment to Joseph? (page 207)   Yes ____ No ____

16. We learn it was another _____ before Joseph was summoned to interpret another dream, however this interpretation would be for Pharaoh, the King of Egypt. (page 208)

Read Genesis 41:17-24 &Genesis 41:29-33 (page 208 & 209)

17. Joseph's interpretation—there would be _____ of plenty followed by _____ of famine, and the famine would utterly deplete the land. (page 209)

18. Joseph went on to suggest that Pharaoh put someone in charge of managing his affairs and gather as much grain into his storehouses during the seven plentiful years as possible. Whom did the King appoint to be over Egypt's food supply and trade routes? (page 209 & 210) _____

CLOSE IN PRAYER — Journal your prayer requests

Notes & Prayers: _____
_____
_____
_____

DAY THREE — Life of Joseph (continued)

Open in Prayer — Invite the presence of the Holy Spirit

Read Genesis 41:39-42 (page 210)

1. Joseph was 30 years old at this time, meaning he had endured _____ of hard practice in order to prepare him for this day. (page 210)

2. One of the main things to remember in the game of life is most of the time we won't know where the Lord is _____. (page 210)

3. For Joseph, all the hardship he endured was for _____ _____ only: to save his family from destruction thus preserving the nation of Israel. (page 210)

4. They had judged Joseph with their _____, and as a result of their sin had tried to determine Joseph's fate. God had another plan. (page 210)

Read Genesis 42:2 & Genesis 42:10-13 (page 211)

5. Jacob learned that Egypt is selling grain, so he sent his sons to secure provisions for the family. _____, they had no clue that the man they were going to be bargaining with was the brother they years earlier had _____. (page 211)

6. When they arrived in Egypt they did not recognize Joseph, but Joseph knew them immediately. He spoke to them through an interpreter so they would assume he would not be able to understand their deliberations. Did Joseph have a plan to trick the brothers? (page 211)   Yes ____ No ____

7. Joseph had planned for them to _____ to their father. In order to keep them _____, they must leave a brother behind in prison and promise to return with the youngest brother, _____. (page 211)

Read Genesis 42:36 (page 211)

8. Jacob, fearful of _____, forbids them to return to Egypt. However, over time the famine continued and became too much for them. Jacob has no choice but to send them back with more money to buy grain and, of course, with _____, as requested. (page 211 & 212)

9. The brothers were wrought with fear and came before Joseph, _____ _____, knowing to return to their father without Benjamin would quite possibly cause his death. (page 212)

10. Joseph decided that he had let them _____ long enough. Not able to hold back any longer, he sends everyone out of the room so he could be alone with his brothers. A weeping Joseph _____ to them. (page 212)

Read Genesis 45:3-8 & Genesis 46:1-4 (page 212 & 213)

11. Joseph had played all the _____. He had spent hours upon hours _____ for this day. When the time came, instead of seeking revenge, he granted his brothers _____. (page 213)

12. We can't fully _____ the Lord and all His ways. Our lives are His to do what he wants, and our part is to simply die to our own agendas by _____ ___ _____ what He is _____ us through life's circumstances. (page 213)

13. God, speaking directly to Jacob, told him not to fear, that He would make him a _____ and that Joseph, "will put his hand on your eyes." Jacob was also named _____, a name God previously bestowed upon him in Genesis 32:28. (page 213)

Review the Actions, Consequences and Lessons found on pages 214-216 and be prepared to discuss. _____
_____
_____
_____
_____

Read Romans 11:29 (page 216)

14. When God has a plan to accomplish something through us, _____ will stand in His way. The calling on Joseph's life was _____, and the calling on your life is _____. (page 216)

15. Like Joseph experienced, life deals us many blows, setting us back. However, without the proper _____, we might not see them as possible opportunities. (page 216)

16. Joseph must have felt very lonely and full of rejection at all that transpired at the hands of his family. But he _____ through it all and his _____ _____ proved effective, eventually leading to the salvation of many. (page 216)

17. Name some other people in the bible that experienced God's practice rounds. (page 217 & 218) _____
_____
_____

18. As a result of their faith and _____, they changed the world. (page 218)

19. Like these men and women, we are also experiencing life, _____, for what God wants to do in and through us. (page 218)

CLOSE IN PRAYER — Journal your prayer requests

Notes & Prayers: _____
_____
_____
_____

DAY FOUR — Relational Practice Rounds / Vocational Practice Rounds

Open in Prayer — Invite the presence of the Holy Spirit

1. The biggest decision you will make in your life is the decision to _____ Jesus Christ into your heart. The second biggest decision most of us will make is _____ the person we will marry and spend the rest of our days with here on earth. (page 218)

2. Have you given consideration to the fact that all the _____ you have entered into are mere _____ in preparation for that one special _____? (page 218)

3. Let's face it, we are all _____ for many, and we are all _____ for that one special person God has set aside for us. (page 218)

4. To all young and old alike, I say embrace the _____, study God's Word and fully prepare. So when the time comes for you to step into your calling, you will have a greater chance at _____. (page 220)

5. Will we _____ our practice rounds until the Lord says it is time for the main event, or will we become _____ in our solitude and take matters into our own hands? (page 220)

6. When we make the decision to find employment in order to provide for our family, do we just wander about aimlessly in hopes that someone will discover our talent and put us to work? (page 221)   Yes ____ No ____

7. Wouldn't it be smart once you get ready to interview to make a short list of companies in your related field and set as many appointments as possible in order to hone your interview skills? (page 221)   Yes ____ No ____

8. You should participate in several interview "_____" with companies that are not at the top of your list. (page 221)

9. This would give you an idea how your resume is perceived, help you to know what questions are going to be asked and assist you in honing your interview skills. (page 221)   True ____ False ____

10. "What if, after all my preparation, I sit for an interview with the one company I desire to work for and they don't extend an offer?" Then you embrace the fact that the Lord was _____ you from making a _____ and _____ _____ you never would have _____ on your own. (page 222)

Read Revelation 3:8 (page 222)

11. If we truly trust that the Lord has our best interests at hand, we can pray specifically for what we think would be best or what we think we want. But, we are freed from _____ if the answer to our prayer is _____ _____ than we had hoped. (page 222)

12. "What if, after all that preparation, the golfer doesn't win the tournament?" What is the answer? (page 222) _____
_____
_____

13. Does not winning in the past keep those golfers from competing in the future? (page 222)   Yes ____ No ____

14. We must persevere, but die in our expectations and trust in the _____ _____ in every area of our life. (page 222)

List some examples of relational and vocational practice rounds you have experienced.
_____
_____
_____

CLOSE IN PRAYER — Journal your prayer requests

Notes & Prayers: _____
_____
_____
_____

DAY FIVE — Practice Rounds of Endurance / Unexpected Practice Rounds

Open in Prayer — Invite the presence of the Holy Spirit

1. Paul reminded us that one of the most important aspects of our Christian walk is to _____ through the ups and downs on this journey we call life. (page 223)

Read Proverbs 29:18 (page 223)

2. Many of our life experiences won't seem like practice rounds preparing us to reach a specific goal or to achieve something better or more important in life. (page 223)
   True ____ False ____

3. We can see that God knew all along the direction we needed to take to be successful. (page 223)   True ____ False ____

Read the story on page 223 and Hebrews 6:13-15 (page 223)

4. He, like Abraham, had _____ and obtained the prize! (page 224)

5. In order for any of us to derive a benefit from our _____, we must stay the course and not _____ until the day that we can say it is done. (page 224)

Practice Rounds • 109

6. We too can have a vision or goal to shoot for and rest assured. If it is the Lord's will, all of our _____ for that day when we are standing on the stage of life with _____ in hand. (page 224)

Read 2 Timothy 4:7-8 (page 224)

7. What was Paul's final declaration as he endured the practice rounds in his life? (page 224)
_____
_____

List some examples of practice rounds of endurance and unexpected practice rounds you have experienced. _____
_____
_____
_____
_____

Read the story under **UNEXPECTED PRACTICE ROUNDS** on page 224 and ending on page 225

8. In life, we don't always know how many _____ we must play, nor do we always get to choose the _____ on which those _____ are played. (page 225)

9. When we put our trust in Jesus Christ, we can overcome any obstacle put in our path. (page 225)   True ____ False ____

10. We can endure through the good times and hard times knowing that our _____ _____ are continued preparation. Preparation for the day the Lord _____ into His service. When He introduces us to our potential _____ _____, helps us reach a _____, or gives us the strength to endure a _____ situation. (page 225)

11. The Lord knows life is hard, and that we must face many _____ moments. He makes use of every situation to protect us, provide for us and, ultimately, prepare us for _____. (page 225 & 226)

12. Regardless, if you know where your journey is taking you, you can trust that God has a plan for your life, a plan that is meaningful and essential to His Kingdom. (page 226)
    True ____ False ____

Read Proverbs 3:5-6 (page 226)

13. When we make a conscious _____, His process of preparation becomes a reality. (page 226)

14. We play the practice rounds in life on God's _____ and with His _____. Until the day we join with Him in Heaven, His _____ is right there coaching us, exposing our flaws, correcting our swing and instructing us. (page 226)

15. Life is one big practice round glittered with many _____ _____, but many _____. (page 226)

16. Prepare, practice and persevere through life, and you too will lift the eternal cup in the air in front of the host of heaven and yell, "_____!" (page 227)

Write examples of practice rounds of endurance and unexpected practice rounds you have experienced. _____
_____
_____
_____
_____

CLOSE IN PRAYER

Summarize what the Lord showed you this week:
_____
_____
_____
_____
_____
_____
_____
_____
_____
_____

WEEK IX
CONCLUSION

DAY ONE — God's Picture Puzzle

Open in Prayer — Invite the presence of the Holy Spirit

Most of us have worked on a large picture puzzle at some point in our life. The puzzle comes in some form of container, and on that container is a picture of the finished puzzle. The picture is the only instruction offered and becomes your road map, so to speak, acting as your guide toward the accomplishment of your goal.

1. Life is a lot like putting that puzzle together. We travel through life trying to find our place in hopes our piece will fit into the _____. (page 229)

2. If everyone has a God-given purpose for being on this planet, wouldn't it make sense that His ultimate goal is to construct His puzzle in such a way that every piece fits perfectly together? (page 229) Yes ____ No ____

3. The family is not one individual, but is made up of a group of individuals, where no member is more important than another. (page 230) True ____ False ____

Reflect on and write the answers to the following: "What role does God calls you to play in family? Why are there pieces missing in our family puzzles?" Be prepared to discuss.
_____
_____
_____

4. The example for family is found in _____. (page 230)

Conclusion • 113

5. The family is meant to be a _____ where we learn how to live _____ with peace and joy. Spiritual family is no different; it is to be a place of _____, where we learn how to live by the _____. (page 231)

Why is there so much division within our natural families, our spiritual families and our societal families? Be prepared to discuss.
_____
_____

Read 1 Peter 5:1-5 & 1 Peter 5:6-8 (page 231)

6. Based on these two passages of scripture would you agree that God desires for us to be part of a strong spiritual family and maintain order within the family structure? Yes ____ No ____

7. Previously, we looked at Proverbs 1:8 where it tells us to obey the "Teaching of the Mother" and the "Instruction of the Father." Why do you think God put it in such a way? (page 232)
_____
_____
_____

8. These roles are not exclusive of one another; the mother and the father are to work together. (page 232)   True ____ False ____

9. Without the proper communication and biblical instruction, parents don't provide the proper example to their children and are running the risk that they will have problems later in life. (page 232)   True ____ False ____

10. Our spiritual legacy can and will live on in our children, so until that time, we don't want to _____. (page 233)

11. There are many _____ kids, kids in _____, kids from _____ homes. (page 233)

12. We learn in Mark 3:33 how Jesus responded to the people by saying, "Who is My mother, or My brothers?" What point was Jesus making in this verse? (Page 233)
_____

13. We are meant to be in family, God's family, where we receive His _____ _____ from the pastoral leadership that He has ordained. (page 233)

14. We are to enter into _____ and hold one another _____ to a holy way of living. (page 233)

15. Men are to be _____ within the church and women are to be _____ within the church. (page 233)

CLOSE IN PRAYER — Journal your prayer requests

Notes & Prayers: _____
_____
_____
_____

DAY TWO — God's Picture Puzzle

Open in Prayer — Invite the presence of the Holy Spirit

1. The church is meant to be a _____, a safe haven, the one place where we can feel _____ through the nurturing body of each of its members. (page 233)

2. Name the three reasons given for the following statement. You have heard it said that the front door of the church is wide open, but so is the back door. (page 233 & 234)
    1) _____
    2) _____
    3) _____

Read Luke 9:49-50 & Matthew 7:21-23 (page 235)

3. These scripture verses are warnings for us in the church today. Leaders will be held _____ unless they truly confess their _____ and _____ in their hearts before the Lord. (page 235)

4. We are all called to be leaders within our Church, personal and business families. Yes ____ No ____

5. Our religious congregations today are made up of people who come from dysfunctional family environments. (page 235)   True ____ False ____

6. Tithing is a controversial subject and creates division among many believers. (page 236)   Yes ____ No ____

7. We are encouraged through God's Word to give the tithe not to the church or to a preacher but to God, without condition. (page 236)   True ____ False ____

8. What do we experience in return when we faithfully give our tithe to God? (page 236)
   _____

Read Malachi 3:8-12, Matthew 23:23-25 & Mark 12:41-44 (pages 236 & 237)

9. The enemy easily ensnares our thinking when we hold onto anything in life that stands in the way of a _____ with the Lord. (page 237)

10. If we aren't willing to give Him everything—our whole livelihood—then we are in bondage to whatever it is we are holding onto. (page 237)   True ____ False ____

Read 2 Corinthians 9:7 (page 238)

11. Based on this scripture what is God's desire for us? _____

12. George Washington, our nation's first president, once said, "Let your heart feel for the _____ of everyone, and let your hand give in _____ to your purse." (page 238)

13. He was instructing people to let the Holy Spirit _____ their conscious minds minds. Hoping they would grasp the _____ that if you are blessed, you are to be a blessing to others. (page 238)

14. People's hearts have become hardened toward the biblical messages they are hearing instead of what God really wants them to grasp. (page 238)   True ____ False ____

15. It is not until we embrace and get involved in _____ and come to an understanding that there is healing in the _____, that God's Word can penetrate and change our hearts. (page 238 & 239)

16. God's eternal puzzle will not be complete until your piece has been set in place. (page 239)   True ____ False ____

CLOSE IN PRAYER—Journal your prayer requests

Notes & Prayers: _____
_____
_____
_____

DAY THREE—PLACING THE TRINITY OVER OUR LIVES

Open in Prayer—Invite the presence of the Holy Spirit

1. It is one thing to understand and even believe in the _____, but it is another thing entirely to place that _____ over your life. (page 239)

2. By placing it over our person, family, business and the society in which we live, we can achieve _____ and have the _____ over our lives. (page 239)

3. To be successful in life, it would make sense that our triangles must remain in balance and have complete unity. (page 239)   True ____ False ____

4. List the three corners of the triangle found on page 239.
   1) _____
   2) _____
   3) _____

5. God will always be at the helm and will flow in and through the other elements. (page 239)   True ____ False ____

6. Assume the company you are working for is intent on increasing its customer base by lowering the cost of its product. The decision is made at corporate to accomplish this by cutting employee salaries. (page 240) Who suffers in this scenario? _____

7. Assume the company is having trouble keeping good people, so it decides to raise customer prices in order to increase the bonuses they are paying top executives. (page 241) Who suffers in this scenario? _____

8. Assume the employees decide to boost their earnings and start conspiring with customers by giving products away in exchange for cash payment under the table. (page 241) Who suffers in this scenario? _____

Take a moment and reflect on your own life. Write some examples how a natural or spiritual family can get out of balance and how you can place the Trinity over your life. Be prepared to discuss. _____
_____
_____
_____
_____

9. In a perfect world, the triangles of our lives would never be out of balance. (page 242)
   True ____ False ____

10. Therefore, by placing the Trinity over every area of your life, you are inviting _____ covering and coming into _____ with the Creator. (page 242)

Conclusion • 117

11. You will naturally experience an eternal blessing: _____
    _____, which God promises for each of His creations. (page 242)

Read Jeremiah 29:11 (page 242)

12. Based on this scripture what are God's thoughts toward us and what does He desire to give us? _____
    _____

CLOSE IN PRAYER — Journal your prayer requests

Notes & Prayers: _____
_____
_____
_____

DAY FOUR — Final Review

Open in Prayer — Invite the presence of the Holy Spirit

1. Being created in God's image, we possess the three distinct characteristics of the Godhead. Can you name them? (page 242) _____, _____ & _____

2. We came to understand that our _____ minds couldn't fully understand an _____ God. (page 242)

3. We looked at Satan's _____ to corrupt our world through the _____ in which we live (page 242)

4. We came to the realization that most of us have been _____ unaware of the effect the enemy's societal decay has had on our nation as a whole. (page 242)

5. We exposed Satan's _____, the method employed in order to fulfill his _____, knowing he was not omnipresent. (page 242)

6. We saw how he used _____ to his advantage by planting an _____ in every heart born from the union between man and woman. (page 242)

7. We looked at how God used Satan's plan against him to create a _____ _____, by which every one of us has the opportunity to choose where they want to spend eternity. (page 243)

118 • Freedom from S.I.N. Study Guide

8. We exposed the enemy's _____; every time Satan attacks a born-again believer and they confess their sins, repent from those sins and turn back to God, Satan is destined to experience _____ . Over and over again, that is his ultimate insanity. (page 243)

9. We showed as a result of S.I.N., we have all become _____ in some way to the societies we live in and have ignorantly _____ the values established by our Founding Fathers. (page 243)

10. We came to realize that most of us are _____ to just play life. We ignorantly follow other people in hopes they won't lead us off the cliff of life, leading to _____ from God. (page 243)

11. We exposed the three primary plays that the enemy has been running successfully for years. Can you name them? (page 243) _____, _____ & _____

12. We explored the concept of _____, which is not a quick fix. We are _____ from sin when we make a true heartfelt decision. A decision to trust in Jesus Christ and our commitment to live for Him as the _____. (page 244)

13. We learned that the Lord's _____ is one directional and regardless of whether we are walking up or down; we will always be traveling upward. (page 244)

14. We defined several of the _____ on the Lord's stairway. (page 244)

15. We then become aware of the fact that our _____ become our object lessons by which we are able to communicate effectively to strengthen others, especially the younger generation. (page 245)

16. We saw how we are all _____ of God's eternal puzzle, though our _____ might be missing a few pieces and appear incomplete. His puzzle will ultimately bear a _____ image, the image He _____ before creation. (page 245)

17. We learned how important it is to place the _____ nature of God over every aspect of our lives in order to maintain proper _____ and experience His blessings for our family, business, church and societal families. (page 245)

18. Like God, we too need to keep the _____. (page 245)

CLOSE IN PRAYER — Journal your prayer requests

Notes & Prayers: _____

_____

Day Five — iUC Questionnaire

Open in Prayer — Invite the presence of the Holy Spirit

Each of us is an "Innately Unique Creation." We have explored in *Freedom from S.I.N.* that each of us have been created with a body, mind and spirit. We explored how God through the Trinity is Father, Son and Holy Spirit, Jesus is the way, the truth and the life, and Satan is out to kill, steal and destroy.

Therefore, we would challenge that each of us also have three unique qualities that we contribute to any endeavor or task we undertake. We created a survey to assist you in getting in touch with those qualities.

iUC Questionnaire — "Innately Unique Creations"

We are devoted to unlocking the innate qualities that each of us possess. This is not a test, but your results will be in direct proportion to the effort you contribute to the survey. Have fun and know that you are uniquely created. Please begin.

There are 22 questions in this survey and will take approximately 30 minutes to complete.

Three Unique Qualities

Each of us has at least three unique innate qualities or attributes that we lend to any endeavor or task we undertake. Please answer these questions quickly. Your first response will be the most accurate.

1. What do you think you were put on this earth to accomplish? *

* Help Note: This could be a vocational calling, it could be a life purpose and/or it could be the reason you were created. Some people will have a hard time answering this question. That is okay. If you can't think of an answer then list a task recently completed.

2. Based on your answer to the previous question list one unique quality or attribute that you lend to any endeavor or task you undertake. *

* Help Note: For example, if a person is a piano player they might list a unique quality as being able to play by ear. Many people can play the piano, but few can play by ear. This is a unique gift they possess.

3. List the second unique quality or attribute that you lend to any endeavor or task that you undertake.
   _____

4. List your third unique quality or attribute that you lend to any endeavor or task.
   _____

Description of Unique Qualities

Define the three unique qualities you listed in the first group of questions.

5. Write your first unique quality or attribute. Now in your own words define in detail what you mean by that quality or attribute. *
   _____
   _____
   _____

* Help Note: Remember we can all be looking out of the same window, but see a different scene. The definition you give for your quality or attribute will be different from someone else's definition for the same quality or attribute.

6. Write your second unique quality or attribute. Now in your own words define in detail what you mean by that quality or attribute.
   _____
   _____
   _____

7. Write your third unique quality or attribute. Now in your own words define in detail what you mean by that quality or attribute.
   _____
   _____
   _____

History

Now close your eyes for a moment and think back over your life. Start with today and reflect back to your childhood. Do you recall times where you have brought these your specific qualities or attributes to bear on a situation and/or task you have been involved?

8. Briefly describe an incident from your past that came to mind and then list how you used your three unique qualities or attributes. *

_____
_____
_____

* Help Note: Take your time and reflect back on the incident before answering.

9. Think about the last time you gave an instruction to someone. Did you use one or more of your unique qualities or attributes?   Yes ____ No ____

10. Reflect back on a recent task you accomplished. Did you utilize anyone or all of your unique qualities or attributes? *
    Please check all that apply:

    ❐ Most definitely
    ❐ Definitely
    ❐ Somewhat
    ❐ Not at all

* Help Note: Think through the task thoroughly before you answer.

You are Uniquely Created

The purpose of this section is to help you explore in further depth how your qualities or attributes make you unique from other people.

11. If your answer to the last question were "Most Definitely", "Definitely" or "Somewhat" would you agree that these three qualities or attributes might be of value?   Yes ____ No ____

12. If you answered "Yes" to the previous question. Why do you think they have value?

_____
_____
_____
_____

13. Repeat your three unique qualities or attributes.

_____
_____
_____

14. Write a sentence using your three qualities or attributes. Start the sentence with "I" *

   _____
   _____
   _____

* Examples:
   1) I *encourage, challenge* and *propel* people to achieve their goals.
   2) I lead by *example, motivate* people to work together and *accomplish* whatever I put my mind to.

15. Again, think back over your life back to your childhood. Would you say that you have been using those three qualities or attributes for most of your life?
    Yes ____ No ____

16. Why is this important for you to know?

    _____
    _____

17. Do you get a good feeling or experience joy when you are operating within these unique qualities or attributes? Yes ____ No ____

18. Do you think it is possible that your qualities or attributes were in you from birth?
    Yes ____ No ____

19. Explain why you choose "Yes" or "No" to the previous question.

    _____
    _____

All of Creation

Are we created beings? Of course, the answer to that question is a resounding, "Yes." How do we know this? We do exist. However, I want to challenge you to a deeper answer. Look all around you, everything you see was created with a unique quality or attribute. Therefore, one might surmise that we were created with a set of unique qualities or attributes.

20. Would you agree that we are all created beings? Yes ____ No ____

21. Since we are all created beings, could it possibly mean that these unique qualities or attributes were created in you as you developed in your Mother's womb?
    Yes ____ No ____

22. You are an "Innately Unique Creation." Thus, is it possible that these qualities or attributes might hold the answer to God's plan or calling for your life?

Yes ____ No ____

Thank you for completing the questionnaire. Be ready to discuss.

CLOSE IN PRAYER

Summarize what the Lord showed you this week:
_____
_____
_____
_____
_____
_____
_____
_____
_____
_____
_____

PLEASE NOTE:

If anyone in your group would like assistance in the discovery process or would like to explore his or her uniqueness in more depth, personal guidance and coaching is available from the author. Please have them contact info@mtoleadership.com to get more information and to set an appointment.

www.ingramcontent.com/pod-product-compliance
Lightning Source LLC
Chambersburg PA
CBHW080346170426
43194CB00014B/2699